THEMATIC UNIT

Jungle

Written by Leigh Hoven

Illustrated by Keith Vasconcelles

Teacher Created Materials, Inc.
P. O. Box 1214
Huntington Beach, CA 92647
© 1990 Teacher Created Materials, Inc.
Made in U.S.A.

ISBN 1-55734-283-0

Table of Contents

Introduction

Jungle contains a captivating whole language, thematic unit. Its 80 exciting pages are filled with a wide variety of lesson ideas and reproducible pages designed for use with intermediate children. At its core are two high-quality children's literature selections, *Why Mosquitoes Buzz in People's Ears* and *A Story, A Story*. For each of these books activities are included which set the stage for reading, encourage the enjoyment of the book, and extend the concepts gained. In addition, the theme is connected to the curriculum with activities in language arts (including daily writing suggestions), math, science, social studies, art, music, and life skills (cooking, physical education, career awareness, etc.). Many of these activities encourage cooperative learning. Suggestions and patterns for bulletin boards and unit management tools are additional time savers for the busy teacher. Furthermore, directions for student-created Big Books and a culminating activity, which allow students to synthesize their knowledge in order to produce products that can be shared beyond the classroom, highlight this very complete teacher resource.

This thematic unit includes:

☐ **literature selections** — summaries of two children's books with related lessons (complete with reproducible pages) that cross the curriculum

☐ **poetry** — suggested selections and lessons enabling students to write and publish their own works

☐ **planning guides** — suggestions for sequencing lessons each day of the unit

☐ **writing ideas** — daily suggestions as well as writing activities across the curriculum, including Big Books

☐ **bulletin board ideas** — suggestions and plans for student-created and/or interactive bulletin boards

☐ **homework suggestions** — extending the unit to the child's home

☐ **curriculum connections** — in language arts, math, science, social studies, art, music, and life skills such as cooking and career awareness

☐ **group projects** — to foster cooperative learning

☐ **a culminating activity** — which requires students to synthesize their learning to produce a product or engage in an activity that can be shared with others

☐ **a bibliography** — suggesting additional literature and nonfiction books on the theme

---

To keep this valuable resource intact so that it can be used year after year, you may wish to punch holes in the pages and store them in a three–ring binder.

Introduction (cont.)

Why Whole Language?

A whole language approach involves children in using all modes of communication: reading, writing, listening, observing, illustrating, experiencing, and doing. Communication skills are interconnected and integrated into lessons that emphasize the whole of language rather than isolating its parts. The lessons revolve around selected literature. Reading is not taught as a separate subject from writing and spelling, for example. A child reads, writes (spelling appropriately for his/her level), speaks, listens, etc. in response to a literature experience introduced by the teacher. In this way, language skills grow naturally, stimulated by involvement and interest in the topic at hand.

Why Thematic Planning?

One very useful tool for implementing an integrated whole language program is thematic planning. By choosing a theme with correlating literature selections for a unit of study, a teacher can plan activities throughout the day that lead to a cohesive, in-depth study of the topic. Students will be practicing and applying their skills in meaningful contexts. Consequently, they will tend to learn and retain more. Both teachers and students will be freed from a day that is broken into unrelated segments of isolated drill and practice.

Why Cooperative Learning?

Besides academic skills and content, students need to learn social skills. No longer can this area of development be taken for granted. Students must learn to work cooperatively in groups in order to function well in modern society. Group activities should be a regular part of school life and teachers should consciously include social objectives as well as academic objectives in their planning. For example, a group working together to write a report may need to select a leader. The teacher should make clear to the students and monitor the qualities of good leader-follower group interaction just as he/she would state and monitor the academic goals of the project.

Why Big Books?

An excellent cooperative, whole language activity is the production of Big Books. Groups of students, or the whole class, can apply their language skills, content knowledge, and creativity to produce a Big Book that can become a part of the classroom library to be read and reread. These books make excellent culminating projects for sharing beyond the classroom with parents, librarians, other classes, etc. Big Books can be produced in many ways and this thematic unit book includes directions for at least one method you may choose.

Why Mosquitoes Buzz in People's Ears
A West African Tale

by Verna Aardema

Summary

The whining mosquito begins the story by complaining to the iguana. The iguana, not wanting to listen, puts sticks in his ears. This starts a series of humorous events involving a variety of jungle animals which ends in the death of an owlet. Mother Owl is so upset that she will not hoot - the signal for night to end. Night continues on and on and on. The jungle animals hold a council meeting to get to the bottom of the problem.

The story is well told with rich, repetitive language, humor, and colorful, award-winning illustrations. Children will naturally join in as the story is read aloud.

Sample Plan

Day 1

- Introduce Attendance Graphing, Math Summary statements, and related activities (pages 36-38).
- Show illustrations in *Why Mosquitoes Buzz in People's Ears* and name the animals and the sounds they make.
- Do Matching Game (page 6, 8, and 9).
- Homework – Create an Animal Sound (page 10).
- Create an Insect (page 11).

Day 2

- Attendance Graphing and related activities (page 36).
- Read *Why Mosquitoes Buzz in People's Ears*.
- Reread story and have students add their sounds from the homework activity; tape for later listening.
- Writing The Whining Mosquito (page 14).
- Do Specimen Report (page 12).
- Make Insect Display Case bulletin board (page 13).
- Learn Contour Drawing (page 15).

Day 3

- Attendance Graphing and related activities (page 36).

- Reread story noting animals' sounds and movements.
- Complete Animal/Action/Sound Chart (page 9).
- Make and play Goin' on a Jungle Walk (pages 16 - 17).
- Make Contour Drawing for Big Book (page 15).
- Homework – Play Goin' on a Jungle Walk with family or friends.

Day 4

- Attendance Graphing and related activities (page 36).
- Reread story listening for the monkey's role.
- Make monkey puppets (page 7).
- Write and perform a monkey dialogue.
- Watercolor contour drawings.

Day 5

- Attendance Graphing and related activities (page 36).
- Write chant (page 19).
- Make Big Book (page 19).
- Chant or Sing Big Book for another class.

Overview of Activities

SETTING THE STAGE

1. Gradually introduce **Attendance Graphing**, **Jungle Log**, **Talk Around**, **Summary Statements**, and **Round Table** (explanation, pages 36-38) to be used daily throughout the unit. Page 38 has specific questions that may be used for the Attendance Graphing.

2. **Introduce the Book** — Show the illustrations of the various animals in the book to the students, but do not read the story. Be sure students know the names of the animals. (You may wish to show realistic pictures to them.) Discuss the sounds these animals may make when they move and when they "speak," but do not read the sounds from the book. Discuss and demonstrate how we may write sounds phonetically.

3. **Matching Game** — Designate partners. Give each pair a copy of pages 8 and 9. Direct the students in the reading of the sounds. (This can be an excellent phonics lesson.) Have each pair follow the directions. Explain that these will be their guesses or predictions. (A second copy of these pages will be used by each pair after they have heard the story.)

4. **Create an Animal Sound** (Homework Activity) — Have students follow the directions on page 10 to find household items to create sounds for animals from the story. Have them fill in the sheet and bring the items to school.

Rabbit		Iguana	
Wooden Spoon rubbed on grater	Shrik-Shrik-	Two pieces of sandpaper rubbed against each other	Mecha-Mecha

5. **Science/Art** — Create an Insect (page 11). Save for Specimen Report and Display Case (see #5 below).

ENJOYING THE BOOK

1. **Read the book** aloud to the entire class. Use lots of expression. Encourage students to join in on the repetitive parts. Don't forget the last page!

2. **Read again** — Have students use the household items to make the sounds they created when their animal is mentioned. This can be taped and played back for a reading with sound effects.

3. **Writing** — Use The Whining Mosquito (page 14).

4. **Art** — Contour Drawing (page 15).

5. **Science**—Specimen Report (page 12). Have students fill this in for the insect they have created. Explain that a scientist who studies insects is an entomologist. Use the reports to make the Display Case Bulletin Board (page 13).

6

Overview of Activities *(cont.)*

ENJOYING THE BOOK (cont.)

6. **Reread** the story, asking students to note the animals' sounds and movements.

7. **Animal Action/Sound Chart** — Have students work with the same partners they had for the Matching Game. They should complete an accurate chart using pages 8 and 9. Have them compare the new chart with their original guesses.

8. **Art** — Contour Drawing for Big Book (page 15).

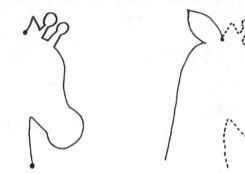

9. **Game** — Make and play Goin' on a Jungle Walk (pages 16-17).

10. **Homework** — Take game home and play with a family member.

EXTENDING THE BOOK

1. **Reread** the story, listening for the monkey's role.

2. **Monkey Dialogue** — Make monkey stick puppets by attaching a craft stick to the monkey pattern on page 39. Or, have students create their own puppets. Patterns for a paper bag puppet are on page 18. Write and perform a dialogue in which the monkey explains (defends) his actions. **Extension:** Have students create the necessary animal puppets to re-enact the meeting of the animal council.

3. **Art** — Watercolor the contour drawing for the Big Book.

4. **Chant** — Introduce and demonstrate the chant for the Big Book (page 19). Have students meet in groups according to the animal they have drawn. Each group should write a verse for the chant and submit it for teacher approval. The approved verse and their animal pictures should be used for the Big Book (directions on page 19).

5. **Culminating Activity** — Share the Big Book and chant with another class, librarian, parents, etc. Add the Big Book to the classroom library.

The Matching Game

Work with a partner. Cut out the boxes below. With your partner try to match the animal, its picture, its action, and its sound. When you have decided, glue your guesses to a copy of page 9. Do this activity before you hear *Why Mosquitoes Buzz in People's Ears* and again afterwards. Compare your answers.

Sample:

| Mosquito | | Whining in People's Ears | Zeee! |

Animal	Picture	Action	Sound
Iguana		bounded	pem, pem, pem
Iguana		screeching and leaping	mek, mek, mek
Python		went off through the reeds	wasawusu
Rabbit		came and sat down	badamin, badamin
Crow		bobbing its head	rim, rim, rim, rim
Monkey		glancing from side to side	nge, nge, nge
All animals		crying	krik, krik, krik
Monkey		slithering	Hoo! Hooooo!
Mother Owl		laughed	kili wili
Lion		hooted	kaa, kaa, kaa

Animal/Action/Sound Chart

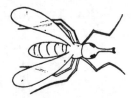

Work with your partner. After reading the story, *Why Mosquitoes Buzz in People's Ears*, use the Matching Game cards (page 8) to create an accurate chart.

Animal	Picture	Action	Sound
Iguana			
Iguana			
Python			
Rabbit			
Crow			
Monkey			
All animals			
Monkey			
Mother Owl			
Lion			

Name_____

Create an Animal Sound

* Select two animals from this list.

Python	**Lion**
Rabbit	**Owl**
Crow	**Owlet (baby owl)**
Monkey	**Iguana**

* Find household items (that you can bring to school) that will make a sound for each of your animals.

* Fill in the chart below.

Animal Sound Chart

❶

Animal Name	**Animal Picture** (you draw)
Household items for sound	Words for the sound

❷

Animal Name	**Animal Picture** (you draw)
Household items for sound	Words for the sound

10

Create an Insect

The Earth's Jungles have over 20,000,000 different types of insects. Many are yet undiscovered and unclassified. Use the following characteristics and your imagination to create an insect. Name it after the scientist that discovered it — You!

* All insects have 3 body parts–head, thorax, and abdomen.

* All insects have 6 jointed legs.

The **Head** has eyes, antennae, and a mouth that sucks or chews.

The **Thorax** has 6 legs (3 on each side) and usually 4 wings. Some wings help an insect fly. Some wings protect. Wings are always symmetrical — one side is the same size, shape, and color as the other.

The **Abdomen** has 10–11 segments. You can usually see 5–8.

Use the patterns below (and/or make some of your own) to create an insect. Trace on construction paper and cut out. Glue together.

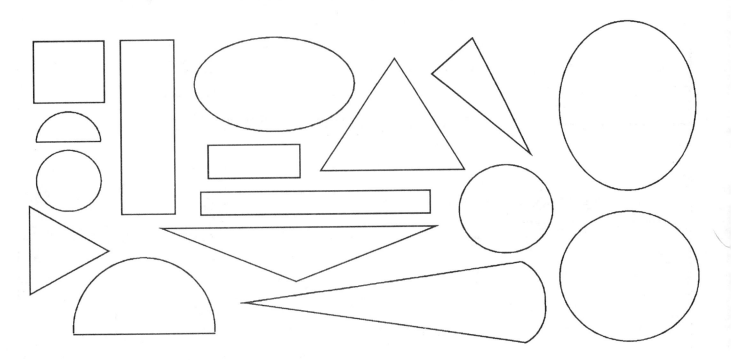

Be sure your insect has 3 body parts and 6 jointed legs.

Add color and details with crayon, markers, tissue paper, etc.

Fill out a Specimen Report (page 12) for your insect.

Why Mosquitoes Buzz in People's Ears

Specimen Report

Use this form to tell about your animal.

After you have completed it, cut off the directions and display it with your animal.

Specimen Report

Type of Animal: _____

Specimen Name: _____

Date of Discovery: _____

Size: _____

Weight: _____

Coloring: _____

_____

_____

Food it eats: _____

How it moves: _____

Natural enemies: _____

_____

Additional Facts:

1. _____

2. _____

Discovered by _____
zoologist

Insect Display Case

Direct students to classify their insects according to a criteria on their Specimen Report. Mount reports with insects to create a colorful and meaningful display. Place sentences at the bottom of the display to reinforce concepts.

CRAWLING GROUP	FLYING GROUP	JUMPING GROUP

All insects have 3 body parts —

head   thorax   and   abdomen.

All insects have 6 legs.

The Whining Mosquito

Write the excuses the mosquito might buzz into someone's ear — for example, " I didn't mean to," or, "They really were very small yams."

Zeee! Is everyone still angry with me?_____

KPAO!

Contour Drawing and Watercolor

Materials

12" x 18" gray or light blue construction paper;

black or white crayon;

set of watercolors

Procedure

1. Look at the giraffe on the page that begins, "At last King Lion called a meeting of the animals."

2. Explain that the contour is the same as the outline, and is the style used by the book's illustrator.

3. Hold the book up so that the students can see the picture. Have them trace the contour of the giraffe in the air with their fingers.

4. Give students a sheet of paper and a white or black crayon.

5. **RULES:** Object must go top to bottom, side to side to fill the paper. You may use only your crayon. No pencils. No erasing. Draw CONTOUR!

6. Draw right side of giraffe.	7. Start at the top again and draw the left side of the giraffe's contour.	8. Add details—jaw line, eye, nose, and spots.
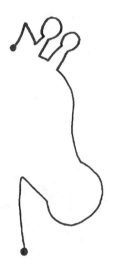	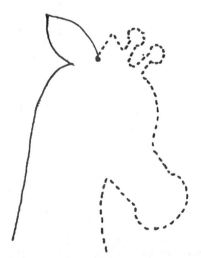	

9. Go over all crayon lines to darken them. Make them at least 1/4" wide.

10. Paint with watercolors. The crayon will resist the paint and contour lines will show up well.

Be the first explorer to witness the animal meeting.

Roll a die. Move along the path following the directions.

Paper Bag Monkey Patterns

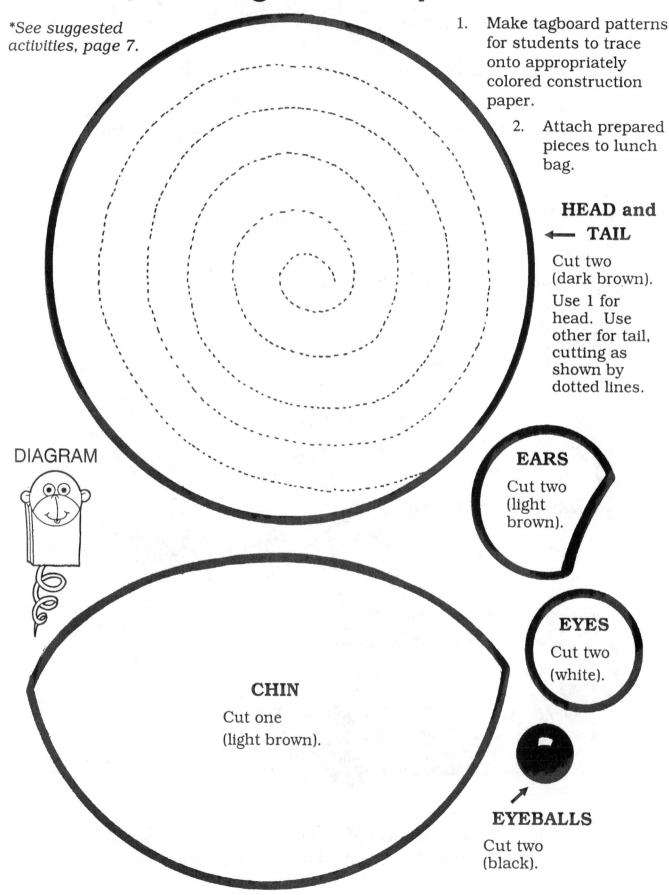

*See suggested
activities, page 7.*

1. Make tagboard patterns
   for students to trace
   onto appropriately
   colored construction
   paper.

2. Attach prepared
   pieces to lunch
   bag.

HEAD and
← TAIL

Cut two
(dark brown).

Use 1 for
head. Use
other for tail,
cutting as
shown by
dotted lines.

DIAGRAM

EARS

Cut two
(light
brown).

EYES

Cut two
(white).

CHIN

Cut one
(light brown).

EYEBALLS

Cut two
(black).

18

The Animal Council

Chant and Big Book

1. Have students select an animal from the story.

2. Do a contour/watercolor of the animal and let dry (directions, page 15).

3. Group students by the animal they select and have each group complete a verse for the chant. (The rhythm of **"Old MacDonald Had a Farm"** is a good guide.)

Chant Opening:
The animal council met one day.

Jibber, Jabber, Jibber, Jabber, Jibber.

To decide the price the mosquito must pay.

Buzz, Zeee, Buzz, Zeee, Buzz.

Verse Frame:
The _____ _____
　　　　　　(2 syllable adjective)　　　　　　　　　(animal)

_____ _____ _____ _____.
(past tense verb)　　　　(prepositional phrase)

_____ _____ _____ _____ _____
　　a　　　　　b　　　　　a　　　　　b　　　　　a
　　　　　　　　　　(sound)

Sample Verse:
The purple pythons slithered

through the vines.

Swish, Hiss, Swish, Hiss, Swish.

Chant Closing:
The council decided since mosquito was wrong,

Jibber, Jabber, Jibber, Jabber, Jibber.

It forever after must sing this song —

Buzz, Zeee, Buzz, Zeee, Buzz.

KPAO! (slap ear)

Hint: This is related to the Matching Game (page 8) and Homework Activity (page 10). Students may refer to them for ideas.

4. Make charts for the chant by cutting out contour animals and gluing to large sheets of paper on which the verse for that animal is written. Make pages for the chant opening and closing. Post around room for reference while performing chant. Assemble a into Big Book for a momento of the unit.

A Story, A Story

by Gail E. Haley

Summary

This book was written and illustrated by Gail E. Haley in 1970. It was awarded the Caldecott Medal for excellence in children's book illustrations.

It is one of many African stories about Ananse the "spider man." These stories crossed the Atlantic Ocean in the ships that brought slaves to the Americas. Their descendants still tell some of the stories today. Ananse or Anansi has become Anancy in the Caribbean Islands and Aunt Nancy in the southern United States.

A Story, A Story tells how stories become the property of the common man. The Sky God owns all the stories and agrees to grant them to Ananse if Ananse can bring him three items — Osebo, the leopard of the terrible teeth; Mmboro, the hornet who stings like fire; and Mmoatia, the fairy whom men never see. Of course, this small, defenseless man outwits all three, captures them, and delivers them to the Sky God.

In the book, you will find many African words. By listening carefully and using context clues, students can figure out their meanings. At times words and phrases are repeated. Africans use this type of repetition to intensify meaning, much as we use "very." For example: "So small, so small, so small" means very, very small.

Sample Plan

Day 1

- Attendance graphing, math summary statements, and related activities (page 36).
- Introduce the book and have children share their favorite stories.
- Read the story, predicting how Ananse will capture each creature.
- Do Lesson I of Big Book activity - "Goin' on a Leaf Hunt" (page 28).
- Introduce and assign homework activity, Ananse Gazette (page 21).

Day 2

- Attendance graphing and related activities (page 36).
- Share homework.
- Use "How Ananse Caught the Fairy" sequencing activity (page 26).
- Do Lesson II of Big Book activity - "Making a Jungle Animal" (page 29).
- Music - "In the African Jungle" (page 53).

Day 3

- Attendance graphing and related activities (page 36).
- Demonstrate how to make a story board (page 26).
- Do Lesson III of Big Book activity - "Creating a New Story" (page 30).

Day 4

- Attendance graphing and related activities (page 36).
- Use art activity "Help Ananse Spin a Web" (page 22).
- Do Lesson IV of Big Book activity - "Making a Story Board" (page 30).

Day 5

- Complete Web Bulletin Board (page 25).
- Make and eat Yummy Yams (page 65).
- Do Lesson V of Big Book activity — "Putting It All Together" (page 31).

Overview of Activities

SETTING THE STAGE

1. Gather the children together so that they are comfortable and can all see the book. The illustrations are an important part of the content and the beauty.

2. Show the title page of the book. Explain that the story is an African folktale. On a map and/or globe show the children where Africa is in relationship to their country.

3. Ask the children to predict what the story will be about. Record those predictions on the chalkboard or chart paper. Later, compare the predictions with what actually happened in the book. Prediction is an important part of comprehension, so this activity is essential.

4. Read the first page of the story: "Once, oh small children round my knee, there were no stories on earth to hear. All the stories belonged to Nyame, the Sky God. He kept them in a golden box next to his royal stool."

STOP... Tell the children briefly what some of your favorite childhood stories were and why you liked them. Have them tell you what their favorite stories are and why. To save time, take only a few volunteers and then have the children turn to their neighbors and tell them. This allows all children to become actively involved and provides opportunity for oral communication. This should not take more than a few minutes.

ENJOYING THE BOOK

1. As you continue to read the book, stop when Ananse encounters each creature, and have the children predict how Ananse is going to trick and capture it.

2. Begin Big Book activity by "Goin' on a Leaf Hunt." See page 28 for Lesson I directions.

   Continue the Big Book preparation by doing a lesson from pages 28-31 each day until the Big Book is completed. This activity allows students to use the language patterns from *A Story, A Story* to create their own illustrated writing.

3. HOMEWORK ACTIVITY: Have students take home the ANANSE GAZETTE (page 23). This will need to be explained and modeled first. There is a section for the student "reporter" to interview his teacher. Role play this with the entire class. Write out your answer so that the students can copy it onto their papers.

Overview of Activities *(cont.)*

4. Duplicate "Help Ananse Spin a Web" (page 24) for each student or student pair. This art activity will lead to a student-created bulletin board. Read over the directions with the students and model the two types of spider webs. Have the book available so students can refer to the text, and provide the listed art materials. This activity may take 40-50 minutes. When all the spider webs are dry, have the students help to create the bulletin boards described on page 25.

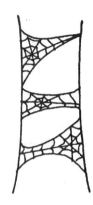

5. COMPREHENSION ACTIVITY: Duplicate the student page "How Ananse Caught the Fairy" (page 27). Have students work in pairs to complete the activity. See teacher directions on page 26.

6. CREATING A STORY BOARD: Students will need to have the correct sequence of sentences from page 27. This is a terrific activity to use with any book or story. It is especially good for this book because the art is exceptional. See teacher information sheet (page 26).

EXTENDING THE BOOK

1. Complete the class Big Book of Ananse stories (pages 28-31). Share this Big Book with another class, the school library, or invited guests before adding it to the classroom library.

2. Compare *A Story, A Story* with other Anansi stories. Read them to the children or have students read and share them with the class. Make a chart to show similarities and differences. (The Joel Chandler Harris *Uncle Remus* stories are variations. See Bibliography, page 79 for other suggestions.)

3. Begin an in-depth study of tropical rain forests using pages 46-63.

4. This study of our endangered tropical forests leads naturally to researching and reporting about endangered species all over our earth. Use pages 67 to 78 to organize this research.

THE ANANSE GAZETTE

Volume I   Date:

Favorite Stories Surveyed by Students at _____

(School Name)

To discover what stories are in the Sky God's golden box, this reporter interviewed teacher, family, and friends.

Reporter: What was your favorite childhood story? Why did you like it best?

Teacher: _____

_____

_____

_____

_____

_____

Family Member: _____

_____

_____

_____

_____

_____

(continued top of next column)

Gazette reporter, seen in above "photo" interviewing family member:

_____

Friend: _____

_____

_____

_____

_____

Gazette Reporter: (that's you) _____

_____

_____

_____

_____

_____

_____

(Survey continued on page 2 if you need more space)

Help Ananse Spin a Web

In the book *A Story, A Story*, Ananse, the Spider man, spins several webs. The first one is a web up to the sky. He uses this web like a ladder and climbs it to see the Sky God.

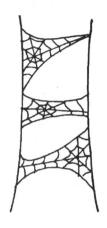

Find this web in the story and study it closely.

At the end of the book, Ananse spins a web around Osebo, Mmboro, and Mmoatia. This bag web helps him carry them up to the sky and set them down at the feet of the Sky God.

Find this web in the story and look at it closely.

Make your own web. You will need:

12" X 18" (30 x 45 cm) sheet of black construction paper; white roving (or string); glue; scissors; silver glitter

Directions

1. Decide which web you will make — ladder or bag.

2. Unravel the roving or string.

3. Draw glue lines as shown on the diagrams.

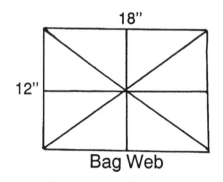

Bag Web

Lay string on glue lines. Cut and glue other pieces of string to form the rest of the web. Use *A Story, A Story* illustrations to help.

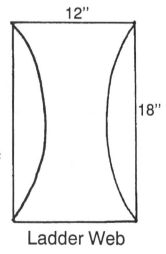

Ladder Web

4. Go over string with a small amount of glue. Sprinkle glitter on the glue and carefully tap off extra.

5. If desired, cut extra paper from outside of the web.

6. Save webs for bulletin boards.

24

Spider Web Bulletin Boards

Ladder Web Board

1. Cover a small box or large mailing envelope with gold foil wrapping paper.

2. Write the names of all the stories that children and family members like on strips of paper. (See homework activity, page 23). Place in gold box.

3. Attach box to top of bulletin board.

4. Place students' web ladders leading up to it.

5. If desired, have students make jungle scenery for background.

Bag Web Board

1. Title the board "What Will Ananse Capture Next?"

2. Cluster the bag webs under the title.

3. Have students make jungle animals to go among the webs. (See page 33 for directions.)

4. Pin animals among the webs so they stick out slightly for a 3-D effect.

5. Have students create names for the animals — for example, leopard-of-the-terrible-teeth or hornet-who-stings-like-fire.

6. Label the animals in the webs.

What Will Ananse Capture Next?

  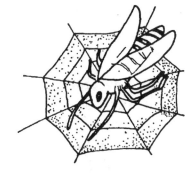

Lion-of-the-mighty-roar   Monkey-who-screeches-shrilly   Hornet-who-stings-like-fire

---

Capturing the Fairy Comprehension Activities

Sequencing Activity

1. Reread the section of the story where Ananse tricks and captures the fairy-whom-no-man-sees. It begins with "Ananse now carved a little wooden doll holding a bowl." It ends "... he carried her to the tree where the leopard and the hornets were waiting." Tell students that they are going to be asked to sequence the events in this section, so they should listen carefully.

2. Put students into workable pairs. As you read the fairy section of the story once more, have the pairs enact the fairy and doll sequence.

3. Distribute page 27 and explain how to do it. If handling 11 items is too much, do the first five together as a class and have the pairs do the rest.

4. With input from each pair, agree as a class on the correct sequence. Do not tell the students if they are right or wrong. If disagreements arise, refer to the text for answers. You will be modeling an important skill.

Creating a Story Board

Materials (*per group*):   12" X 18" (30 x 45 cm) sheets of white drawing paper; sequence strips from How Ananse Caught the Fairy (page 27); white glue; crayons, markers, and colored pencils

Procedure:

1. Divide students into groups of 6. Use the pairs from the sequencing activity and group 3 sets. Give each pair a sheet of paper so that each group has 3 pieces of paper.

2. Have the students fold each of the three 12" X 18" papers into fourths and number the boxes 1-12.

3. In the first box have them write the title, "How Ananse Caught the Fairy," and their names.

4. Have students glue their sentence strips onto the story boards in the correct sequence.

5. The pairs should work together to illustrate each section. Encourage them to fill the spaces. Have them refer to the text when they wish. Students should try to duplicate the illustrator's style. Allow 45 minutes to an hour for this activity. Circulate and praise students who are filling in the entire box and creating an interesting background. You will get great results!

6. Attach sheets with tape and display. Fold accordion style to add to classroom library.

How Ananse Caught the Fairy

Working with a partner, cut apart the sentences below. Arrange them in correct order. Be sure you and your partner agree.

Cut along lines.

(A)   The fairy pushes the doll with her feet, and her feet stick.

(B)   Ananse filled the bowl with yams.

(C)   The fairy sees the doll.

(D)   Ananse then takes the fairy, the leopard, and the hornets to the Sky God.

(E)   The fairy thanks the doll for the yams.

(F)   The fairy slaps the doll again and the other hand sticks.

(G)   Ananse put the doll under the flamboyant tree and hid behind a bush.

(H)   Ananse carved a doll holding a bowl.

(I)   The fairy slaps the doll and her hand sticks.

(J)   When the doll doesn't answer, the fairy gets angry.

(K)   The fairy eats the yams.

A Big Book for *A Story, A Story*

Lesson I, Part 1 - Goin' on a Leaf Hunt (a math/science activity)

Materials: Goin' on a Leaf Hunt student sheet (page 32), one per child;

several shades of green, yellow, purple crayons (peeled, fat crayons work best);

5-10 different types of leaves (relatively fresh, can be rotated through the groups, but tend to become too limp and flat after 15-20 rubbings)

Procedure:

1. Give each child a collection bag. Take class outside for a guided leaf hunt. Tell the children to collect a variety of leaves.

2. After returning to the classroom, discuss the shape, color, edges, etc. of collected leaves and make a chart on the chalkboard or large paper. This will become a Word Bank for the next step.

3. Give each child a "Goin' on a Leaf Hunt" paper (page 32) and a piece of scrap paper.

4. Demonstrate how to make a crayon rubbing. Practice with scrap paper. a) Put leaf down under paper with the vein side up. b) Hold down paper with one hand. c) Rub side of crayon across paper using medium pressure until the leaf print is clear.

5. Have students select one leaf and do a rubbing of it on the "Goin' on a Leaf Hunt" paper. Save other leaves.

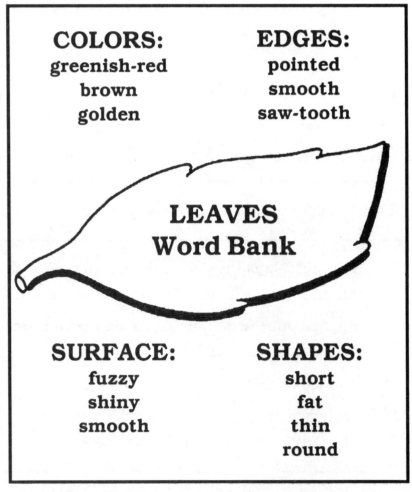

COLORS:
greenish-red
brown
golden

EDGES:
pointed
smooth
saw-tooth

**LEAVES
Word Bank**

SURFACE:
fuzzy
shiny
smooth

SHAPES:
short
fat
thin
round

6. Students then complete the page independently by referring to the WORD BANK.

A Big Book *(cont.)*

Lesson I, Part 2 - Creating a Jungle (a cooperative art activity)

Materials: One sheet 12" X 18" (30 X 45 cm) plain newsprint for each group

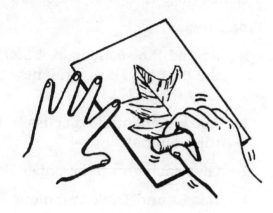

Procedure:

1. Divide students into groups of 4 or 5.

2. Give each group one sheet of newsprint.

3. Have them work together to make leaf rubbings that fill the paper. They may overlap. Use a variety of leaves and colors. *Note: They should work very carefully. The paper is thin and may tear. If tears occur, just tape the back.

4. Collect and save the filled papers for Lesson IV.

Lesson II - Making a Jungle Animal (a cooperative art activity)

Materials: See 3-D Animals, page 33

Procedure:

1. Each group decides on a jungle animal that would be difficult to catch. Each child in the group makes that animal. Record the decisions to make sure each group has chosen a different animal.

2. Demonstrate the making of 3-D animals (directions page 33). Encourage students to use directions as a starting point and be creative.

3. While they are working, have students discuss how Ananse might trick and capture their animals. This will be used in the next lesson. It could also be assigned as a writing activity for homework.

4. Collect and save animals.

A Big Book (cont.)

Lesson III - Creating a New Story (a cooperative language arts activity)

Preparation: Read Round Table technique (page 37).

Materials (for each group):   One How to Catch a _____ (page 34) paper; one pencil

Procedure:

1. Reread the sections in *A Story, A Story* where Ananse captures the leopard and the hornet. Have students recall the sequencing activity for the capture of the fairy (page 27).

2. Allow students to discuss in their groups the method and steps needed to capture their animal.

3. Give each group the paper How to Catch a _____ (page 34) and **one** pencil.

4. Use Round Table technique to have each group write the eight-sentence sequence to capture their animal.

5. Students should edit their sequence to reflect the writing style of the book; i.e., repetition of words for emphasis and multi-part animal names (hippo-in-the-sucking-mud).

Lesson IV - Making a Story Board (a cooperative language arts activity)

Materials (for each group):   two sheets of 12" X 18" (30 X 45 cm) paper;

animals from Lesson II

Procedure:

1. Students write their 8 sequence sentences on the two sheets of paper which have been divided into 4 sections each, as shown.

2. Students illustrate the sentence in each box. Be sure students fill each box. They may be cut apart to make them easier to work on. (You can review the story boards from How Ananse Caught the Fairy, if necessary.) Students should use their 3-D animals in the illustrations, saving one.

A Big Book *(cont.)*

Lesson V - Putting It All Together

Materials (for each group):   Leaf rubbing paper from Lesson I

Story board from Lesson IV

Extra 3-D animal from Lesson II

Two sheets of 18" x 36" (45 X 90 cm) butcher paper

Procedure:

1. Glue the extra 3-D animal to the leaf rubbing jungle scene.

2. Fold butcher paper accordion fashion into three 12" X 18" (30 X 45 cm) sections.

3. Mount leaf rubbing jungle scene on first section, scenes 1-4 of the story board on the second section, and scenes 5-8 on the third section.

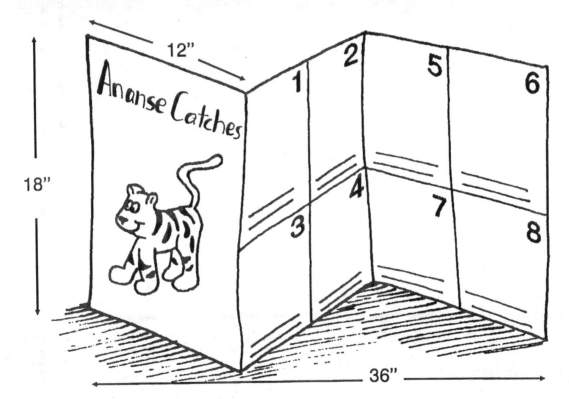

4. Add the title and authors to the front page.

5. Have groups share their stories.

6. If possible, display stories around the room so students can "read the walls" during silent reading.

7. Later, combine all pages (tape together on the back) into a class Big Book. Make an extra leaf rubbing jungle scene for the front cover and title it "ANANSE STORIES by room #____." Keep the Big Book for classroom reading.

Goin' on a Leaf Hunt

You need to find 3 to 5 different types of leaves. They need to be fresh. Do not pick them off bushes and trees without permission.

In the box, make a rubbing of your favorite leaf. (Your teacher will show you how to do this.)

start here

1
2
3
4
5
6
7
8
9
10
11
12
13
14
15

MY LEAF

My leaf is _____ cm long and _____ cm wide.

The color of my leaf is _____.

The shape of my leaf is _____.

The edge of my leaf is _____.

I can see _____ of veins in my leaf.
                              (number)

My leaf is/is not symmetrical. _____

My leaf is from a _____ tree.

3-D Animals

Materials for Four-legged Animals

One 4" X 5 1/2" (10 X 14 cm) piece of construction paper for body; one 2" X 3" (5 X 8 cm) piece of construction paper for head; scraps of construction paper — all colors; scraps of yarn and string — many colors; scissors; crayons or markers; white glue or paste

Procedure for Four-legged Animals

1. Body - Fold the 4" X 5 1/2" construction paper in half, widthwise. Cut out a half-oval from the center of the open edges as illustrated.

2. Head - Fold the 2" X 3" paper in half either lengthwise or widthwise. Cut as illustrated.

   Add details with crayons, markers, paper scraps, yarn, string, etc. to head and body.

3. Glue head to body.

Variations: Stand-Up Animal

After cutting the half-oval in Step 1 above, open the paper and lay flat. Cut 1/2" (1 1/4 cm) slit on each side of the center fold as shown. Fold up along each side to make the legs. Now it can stand up.

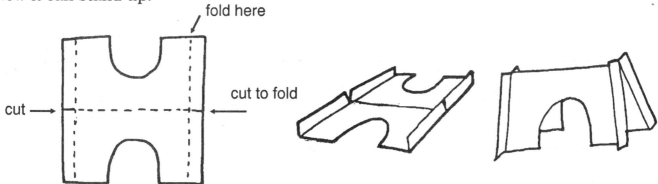

Variations: Other Animals

For birds, reptiles, insects, fish, etc., vary the technique to match the body shape of the animal. For example, a crocodile might begin with a 5 X 8" (12.5 X 20 cm) piece of construction paper folded in half lengthwise.

How to Catch a

_____

1. **The Sky God laughed: "Twe, twe, twe. The price of my stories is that you bring me** _____ .

   _____

2. _____

   _____

3. _____

   _____

4. _____

   _____

5. _____

   _____

6. _____

   _____

7. _____

   _____

8. _____

   _____

Jungle Poetry

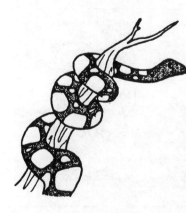

From *Where the Sidewalk Ends*

Three poems from Shel Silverstein's *Where the Sidewalk Ends* are about jungle animals. The well-loved *"Boa Constrictor"* is a hilarious poem to memorize and recite with actions and expression! *"The Toucan"* and *"Instructions"* (for bathing an armadillo) may inspire children to write their own poetry using the patterns and ideas of these two poems. For example, how about a poem entitled *"Instructions for Bathing a Porcupine!"*

From *The Random House Book of Poetry for Children*

Jack Prelutsky's *The Random House Book of Poetry for Children* is an excellent collection of poems on almost any subject. Several of its poems are appropriate for this unit.

You may wish to read *"When Mosquitoes Make a Meal"* by Else Holmelund Minarik in connection with *Why Mosquitoes Buzz in People's Ears*.

"Green Stems" by Margaret Wise Brown may help children imagine the point of view of the creepy crawlies that live on the floor of the rain forest. Have your class write stories about a specific small creature that makes its home there.

Jungle animals are popular topics for poems. Jack Prelutsky's collection includes *"The Boa*,*"* which comments on the size of a boa constrictor. *"The Crocodile"* would be good to use with the Jungle Vine Swing activity on page 44. *"What in the World?"* is a riddle poem by Eve Merriam which includes a verse about chimpanzees. Children will enjoy creating their own riddles using the rhyming-verb pattern of this poem.

A funny poem about spelling a tropical fruit is *"Banananananananana"* written by William Cole.

Here is a good poem for writing variations:

Bug in a Jug	Rhyming Pattern	Word Pattern
Curious fly,	A	Adjective noun
Vinegar jug,	B	Adjective noun
Slippery edge,	C	Adjective noun
Pickled bug.	B	Adjective noun

Anonymous

Variation:

Overheated hippo,
Inviting pool,
Muddy water,
Wonderfully cool.

Daily Writing Activities

Name Magnet

Make name magnets for each child.

Directions and patterns on page 39.

Note: *If you do not have a chalkboard or other area for magnets, use sticky notepaper instead of name magnets.*

Attendance Graphing

Before the children arrive each day, write a question on the board. As students enter the room, they move their name magnet from the holding zone to answer the question. (See diagram below.) This is called attendance graphing since the absent students' magnets will be left in the holding zone.

Holding Zone	What would you rather be?
Jack	monkey ☐ ☐ ☐ ☐ ☐ ☐ ☐
Jill	tiger ☐ ☐ ☐ ☐ ☐ ☐ ☐ ☐

*See suggested questions page 38.

Jungle Log

Have each student make a booklet by stapling the Jungle Log cover (page 40) to several sheets of writing paper. Students should write and elaborate on their answer to each day's attendance graphing question. The writing may be illustrated. This is a quiet activity to use while taking roll, collecting homework, etc. Allow at least 10 minutes.

Talk Around

In groups of 3 to 5, students take turns sharing their log entries and showing their illustrations. Simple rules should be followed:

1. Only one person speaks at a time.

2. Everyone has eye contact with the speaker.

3. Each person has a turn and must speak loudly enough for everyone in the group to hear.

   Doing a Talk Around daily gives students excellent practice in listening and speaking and makes sure their writing has an audience. It also gives children a chance to know one another better — an opportunity which is good for class unity and pride.

Daily Writing Activities *(cont.)*

Mathematical Summary Statements

Students write sentences about the day's attendance graph. Each sentence must contain a mathematical concept.

For example: Seven students would rather be monkeys.

More students would like to be tigers.

One less student would rather be a monkey.

A greater number of students would rather be tigers.

Not acceptable: I would like to be a monkey.

Monkeys are better than tigers.

Tigers weigh more than monkeys.

These may be written as word problems and traded for solving. For example, "How many more students would rather be tigers than monkeys?" This activity is good to use for 10 or 15 minutes at the beginning of a math period.

Round Table (a cooperative learning technique)

After students understand and can apply summary statements, use this procedure.

1. Divide students into groups of 3-5.

2. Each group has one piece of paper and one pencil.

3. The teacher sets a time limit and gives a signal for all groups to begin. The first person in each group writes a math summary statement then passes the paper and pencil to the next person. When the second person is finished writing a summary statement, he/she passes it to the third person, and so forth.

4. The paper goes "round the table" as many times as possible before the signal is given to stop. Each group counts and records the number of summary statements written.

5. Collect all papers. Using the paper with the greatest number, read the statements and determine as a class if they are accurate.

6. Encourage the group with the most statements to share why they succeeded. Record techniques on a chart. Students will learn that cooperation = success.

Daily Writing Activities *(cont.)*

Jungle Log Suggestions

General Ideas:

1. Would you rather be a monkey or a tiger?

2. Would you rather be an anteater or an ant?

3. Would you rather live in a jungle or on an Alaskan island?

4. If you were an animal, would you rather live in the jungle or the zoo? (Consider safety, availability of food, freedom, etc.)

5. Would you rather be a parrot, a piranha, or a python?

6. Would you rather be a botanist (study plants), an entomologist (study insects), or an ichthyologist (study fish)?

Related to *Why Mosquitoes Buzz in People's Ears*:

1. Use on Day 1 — Would you rather be an ant, a grasshopper, or a mosquito?

2. Use on Day 2 — Where did you find the objects for your animal sounds? Show students how to use this type of diagram to answer questions. Be sure that they understand that the overlapping area means both.

3. Use on Day 3 — Have you been stung or bitten by one of these?

4. Use on Day 4 — Which animal in the story did you think was the most foolish? (mosquito, iguana, crow, python)

5. Use on Day 5 — Which animal in the story did you think was the most foolish? (owl, rabbit, monkey, iguana)

Related to *A Story, A Story*:

1. Use on Day 1 — Which story do you like best? (Three Little Pigs, Three Billy Goats Gruff, The Gingerbread Man, Hansel and Gretel)

2. Use on Day 2 — What bait would you use to catch a fairy that no man has ever seen? (honey, tiny fur coat, roses, hamburger)

3. Use on Day 3 — Which do you think would be hardest to catch? (hornet, leopard)

4. Use on Day 4 — If you could build a spider web ladder, where would it take you? (top of Mt. Everest, top of Jack's beanstalk, the moon)

5. Use on Day 5 — Which character do you think was the most foolish? (hornet, leopard, fairy)

Related to Endangered Species report writing:

1. Which do you think is the best way to protect an endangered species? (preserve natural environment, capture and raise offspring in zoos)

2. You can write one letter to an important person urging them to protect the rain forest. Who will you write to and why? (The President of the United States, the Secretary of the United Nations, the head of the government where the rain forest is located, the head of a company that is destroying the rain forest, etc.)

38

Patterns

Reproduce this pattern or the small monkey below onto construction paper or tagboard. Have each child cut the pattern out and write his name on it. A magnetic strip should be attached to the back. (Three-foot magnetic strips are available in craft stores. They can be cut with scissors and have a sticky side which adheres easily.)

Use the large monkey for a stick puppet described on page 7.

Stick Puppet

Name Magnet

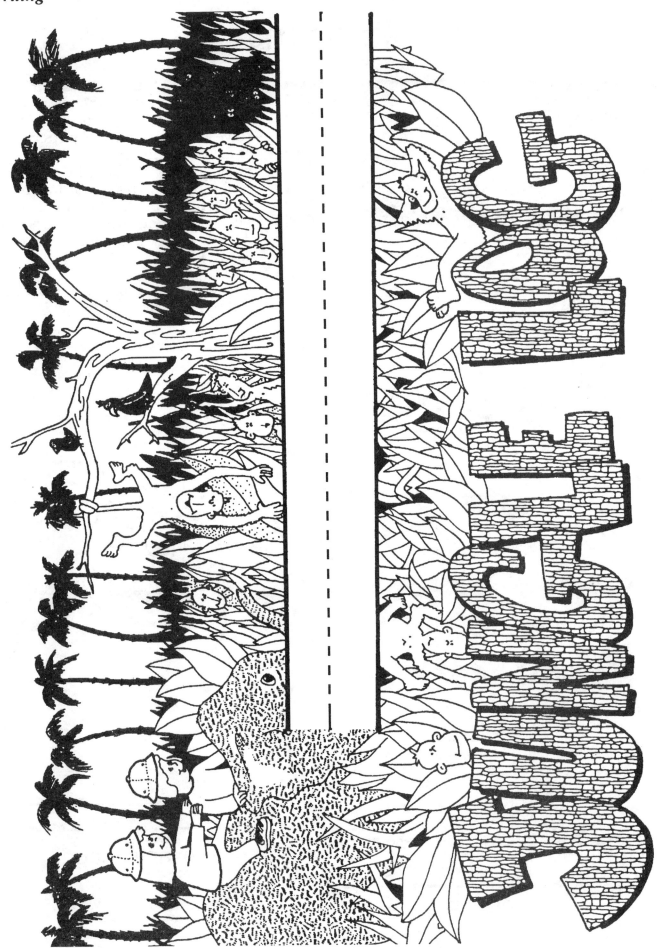

Venn Diagram Compositions

Students will compare and contrast monkeys and elephants and end by writing a five paragraph composition.

Lesson I: Writing About Monkeys

Preparation: Draw a large monkey on chart paper. Gather pictures and books about monkeys.

Procedure:

1. Display chart and pictures.

2. Lead a discussion about monkeys. If students lack background information, read to them about monkeys, then continue the discussion.

3. Put phrases and words students give you on the monkey chart.

have long tails   are mammals

have fur   are playful

like bananas   live in trees

live in the jungle   swing in trees

4. Demonstrate writing a topic sentence and three supporting sentences using the information from the class chart. For example: Monkeys are very playful animals. They live in trees. They swing in the trees with their long tails. Often they eat bananas while swinging.

5. Students then copy (or create their own) topic sentence and add three supporting sentences of their own.

6. Save students' papers and chart.

Lesson II: Writing About Elephants

Preparation: Draw a large elephant on a chart. Collect elephant pictures and books.

Procedure: Follow steps 1-6 from Lesson I, substituting elephants for monkeys.

Venn Diagram Compositions *(cont.)*

Lesson III: Analyzing Similarities

Preparation: Display monkey and elephant charts side by side. Draw two large intersecting shapes on another chart for a Venn Diagram. Supply blank paper to each student.

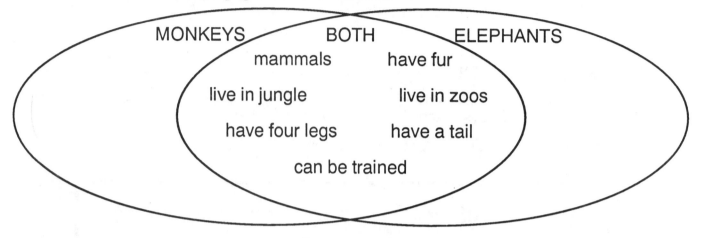

MONKEYS   BOTH   ELEPHANTS

mammals   have fur

live in jungle   live in zoos

have four legs   have a tail

can be trained

Procedure:

1. Reread each previously completed chart with students.

2. Circle the items that are alike.

3. Have students draw two intersecting shapes on their papers to match your chart.

4. Record like items in the center of the new chart and have students copy onto their papers.

5. Have students provide more similarities to add to the chart.

6. Give students this topic sentence: There are many ways that elephants and monkeys are alike. Have them use the Venn Diagrams to write three supporting sentences.

7. Share paragraphs in small groups.

8. Save charts and paragraphs for lessons IV and V.

Lesson IV: Analyzing Differences

Preparation: Display monkey, elephant, and Venn Diagram charts again.

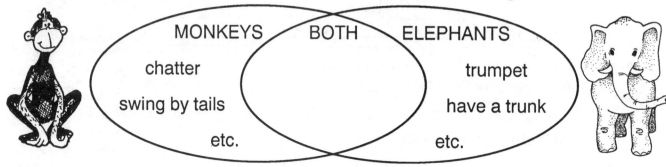

MONKEYS   BOTH   ELEPHANTS

chatter   trumpet

swing by tails   have a trunk

etc.   etc.

Venn Diagram Compositions *(cont.)*

Lesson IV *(cont.)*

1. Reread items on each chart that are not circled. These should be differences. Record differences on Venn Diagram (see bottom of page 42).

2. Pass out students' Venn Diagrams.

3. Students record differences from the chart onto their own Venn Diagrams.

4. Have students discuss parallel ideas such as sounds the animal makes, size of animals, and ways the animals move.

5. Give topic sentence: Monkeys and elephants may be alike but they are also very different.

6. Model a few supporting sentences for the group. They need to have an elephant and monkey parallel reference in each sentence. (For example: Elephants trumpet and monkeys chatter. Elephants have a trunk and monkeys don't).

7. Students write their own paragraph.

8. Share paragraphs. Save paragraphs for Lesson V.

Lesson V: A Five-Paragraph Composition

Preparation: Have class complete Attendance Graph and journal entry — "Would you rather be a monkey or an elephant?" (See page 36.) Display Venn Diagram chart.

Return student paragraphs from Lessons I-IV

Procedure:

1. Have students edit their paragraphs and arrange them in the following order:

     Paragraph 1: Monkeys

     Paragraph 2: Elephants

     Paragraph 3: Monkeys and elephants are alike.

     Paragraph 4: Monkeys and elephants are different.

     Paragraph 5: I would rather be a monkey than an elephant (or vice versa).

   If desired, demonstrate editing so all sentences do not sound the same.

2. Students should now make a final copy of all their paragraphs in one complete composition.

3. Students may illustrate and prepare covers for their compositions.

Extensions: Write a story about your life as a monkey or an elephant. You may use Curious George books by Hans A. Rey or Babar books by Jean de Brunhoff as models.

Jungle Vine Swing
(a suggested homework activity)

Materials: Jungle Vine Swing paper (page 45); 10 or more toothpicks

Background: This is a variation of the old Chinese game of Nim. There is a definite strategy. Students need to play many times to come to a method of winning every time. Be sure to allow enough practices so this does happen.

Procedure:

* Tell the children that they must swing across the crocodile-infested river to safety. There are 10 vines hanging from the tree. Two people take turns swinging (taking one or two vines per turn). The person who swings on (takes) the last vine wins.

* Put 10 toothpicks across the page so that they hang from the tree.

* Players take turns taking one or two toothpicks (vines) each turn.

* No one may skip a turn.

* The person that takes the last toothpick (vine) is saved from the crocodile in the river and wins the game.

Parent Hint:	When you and your child begin to see patterns and possible strategies, work together to see if you can figure out a way to win every time.
Another Hint:	Start with 5 toothpicks and add more each time to figure out a strategy.

Extended learning:

* Add more than 10 "vines" — maybe 12 or 16.

* Try picking up 1, 2, or 3 "vines" each time.

Jungle Vine Swing

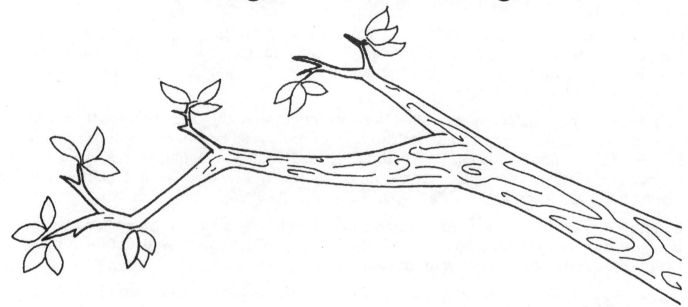

Arrange 10 toothpicks (vines) to hang from tree left to right.

Studying the Tropical Rain Forest

Jungles are dense growths of trees and other vegetation thriving in tropical regions. They are usually a part of a larger area of rain forest. In a jungle, light is able to reach the ground level, causing profuse, tangled vegetation there. Explorers often must cut a path in order to walk through a jungle.

The larger areas of tropical forests, called rain forests because they receive more than 100 inches (250 cm) of rain per year, have fairly clear ground areas because the tall trees shut out the light to the floor of the forest. These forests are located in climatic areas where hot temperatures are nearly constant year-round, so the trees, shrubs, and plants that comprise them are green and lush all year.

The rain forests are one of the richest regions on the earth. As many as five million plants, animals, and insects (about 50 per cent of all living things!) live there. Most of them have not yet been discovered, studied, and named.

Use pages 47 to 63 to help your students learn more about the rain forests and what is happening to them. You will find where these forests are located, why they are disappearing, and what problems this is causing for our planet.

To enhance your study of the jungle, you may wish to do one or more of the following activities:

1. Make a class rain forest mural. Use pages 48, 50, and 51 to help.

2. Plant your own rain forest in an aquarium. See page 49 for directions.

3. Turn your classroom into a rain forest. Turn up the heat and run a vaporizor to simulate the heat and humidity. Use fat green yarn with attached construction paper leaves and flowers to drape the walls and lights with "vines." Use carpet tubes and painted cutouts from appliance boxes to make giant trees.

4. Create a poster with a "Save the Rain Forests" theme.

5. As a class, make a newspaper called *The Jungle Journal*. Include factual articles about the rain forests, an editorial about why they should be saved, want ads for endangered species of jungle plants and animals, etc.

6. Write for information about rain forests and what you can do to help save them. The following organizations provide such information if you include a stamped, self-addressed envelope:

Nature Conservancy International
1800 North Kent Street, Suite 800
Arlington, VA 22209

Creating Our Future
398 North Ferndale
Mill Valley, CA 94941
Ask for "How to Organize a Rainforest Awareness Week at Your School."

Rainforest Information Centre
PO Box 368
Lismore, NSW 2480
Australia

Rainforest Action Network
300 Broadway, Suite 28
San Francisco, CA 94133

46

The Earth's Green Belt

Tropical rain forests cover about 5% of the world's surface. There are three main rain forest regions on three different continents. Study the map. Color it and answer the questions below.

Color the South American and Central American rain forest area light green.

Color the African rain forest (including the island of Madagascar) dark green.

Color the Southeast Asian rain forest yellow.

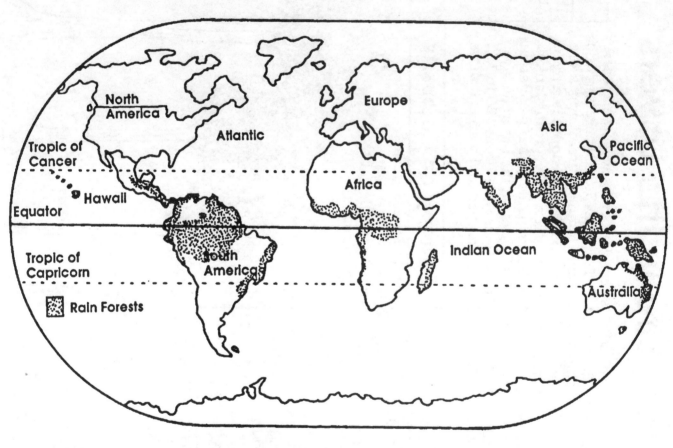

1. The world's rain forests are near what imaginary line?_____

2. The world's largest rain forest is located on which continent? _____

3. Which rain forest is located mostly on islands? _____

4. Why do you think there are almost no rain forests north of the Tropic of Cancer or south of the Tropic of Capricorn? _____

_____

_____

_____

_____

Plant Life in the Layers

A rain forest is made up of four layers. The FLOOR is very dark and always wet. There is very little wind and very little change in temperature. The UNDERSTORY gets a little more sunlight and just a little less moisture. Wind and temperature changes are limited due to the thick canopy above. The UMBRELLA LAYER (or **canopy**) is almost a continuous layer of green. When seen from the air, it looks like a large, green blanket. There is sunlight above, but near darkness below. The few trees that break through the umbrella layer and escape into the sunlight, form the TOP LAYER. These trees range from 120 to 150 feet tall and have a shallow root system. They need to be propped up by an extensive above-ground root system or buttress.

The SOIL of a rain forest is thin and poor. As leaves fall and decay their nutrients are immediately needed for the dense vegetation. Roots absorb them and send them back up to feed the leaves and flowers. The recycling is fast. Fallen leaves in a rain forest do not have time to form deep soil as they do in the forests of North America. There is no winter rest period. The weather changes very little around the equator and the plants are constantly working.

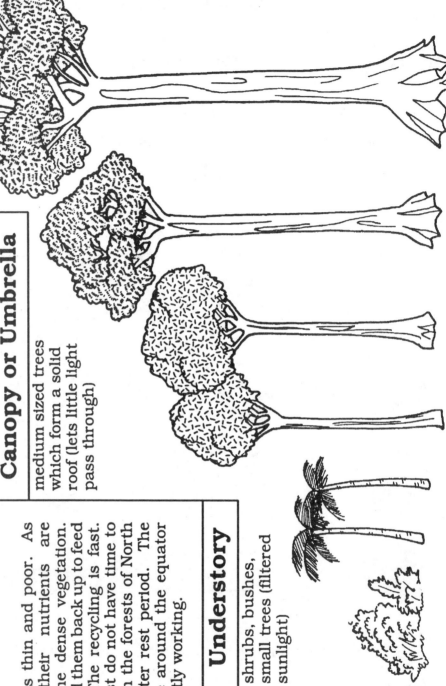

Top Layer

(Penthouse) 120-150 ft. trees (full sun)

Canopy or Umbrella

medium sized trees which form a solid roof (lets little light pass through)

Understory

shrubs, bushes, small trees (filtered sunlight)

Floor

flowers, ferns, decaying material (very dark)

Rain Forest Science Experiment

Materials: plant cutting such as creeping Charlie, spider plant, philodendron; glass of water; large, clear jar big enough to fit over the glass; two thermometers.

Directions:

1. Put the cutting in the glass of water and allow it to root. Make a chart of the daily growth of the root system. (It takes about a week for this part of the activity.)

2. Put an inverted jar over the cutting in the glass of water. Place in the sunlight.

3. Put a thermometer inside the jar to monitor the temperature. Put another thermometer beside the jar to monitor the difference between the outside temperature and the temperature inside the jar. WAIT ONE HOUR.

Answer the following questions:

1. What happens to the temperature inside the jar?

   Why do you think that is?

2. What happens to the water inside the jar?

   Why do you think that happens?

HINT: The jar works the same way as the UMBRELLA LAYER in a rain forest. It traps the moisture and the heat.

   * After the experiment, plant your cutting in a moist, shaded area and watch it grow or keep it as a classroom plant.

Extension: Use an aquarium with a glass lid to plant your own self-watering "rain forest."

Materials: A large aquarium; gravel; charcoal; rich soil; small stones; plants

Directions: Layer gravel and then charcoal (both available at an aquarium shop) on the bottom of the tank.

Spread small stones over the gravel charcoal layer; create small hills and valleys.

Cover the stones with about an inch of soil.

Dampen the compost with water and plant the greenery.

Cover the aquarium with a glass top (or plastic wrap). Keep in a warm spot out of direct sunlight.

You may have to add a little water every few months.

Animal Life in the Layers

Animal life will vary from rain forest to rain forest. On this page and page 51 you will find some of the more common animals who make their homes in each rain forest layer. Research these animals to color them correctly and complete the chart on page 52.

Top Layer

Harpy Eagle

Proboscis Monkey

Hawk

Morpho Butterfly

Umbrella Layer

Porcupine

Spider Monkey

Toucan

Three-toed Sloth

50

Animal Life in the Layers *(cont.)*

Use with pages 50 and 52.

Understory

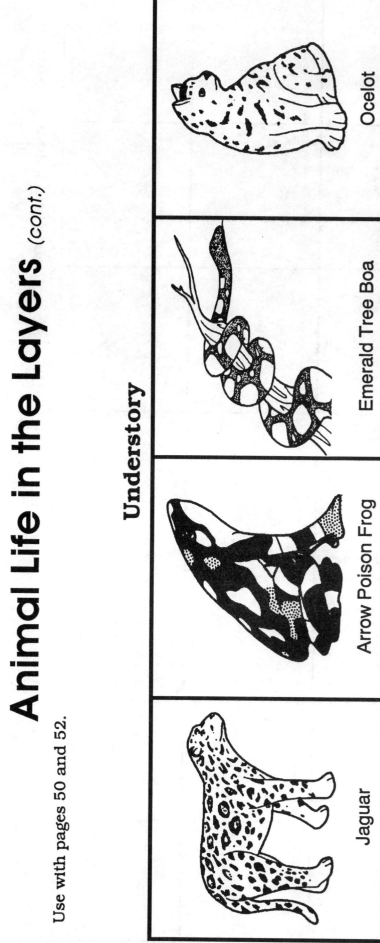

Ocelot

Emerald Tree Boa

Arrow Poison Frog

Jaguar

Across the Curriculum

Floor

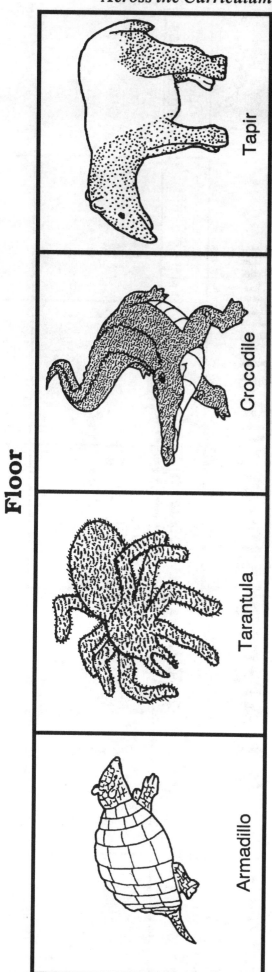

Tapir

Crocodile

Tarantula

Armadillo

© 1990 Teacher Created Materials, Inc.

51

283 Thematic Unit – Jungle

Layers of Life Animal Chart

Animal	Layer	Classification	Appearance	Food	Enemies	Special Characteristics

Teacher note: This can easily be expanded into a bulletin board and used for oral and written language, science, art, etc. Have students make the animal column into a 3-D art project (see page 33) for a more colorful and interesting effect.

52

In the Jungle

Use this activity to review the locations and animals of the rain forest.

Begin by saying to the class:
>Let's travel to the African rain forest.
>In which direction will we travel?
>Which ocean will we cross?

Sing to the tune of "*Old MacDonald*":
>*Refrain:* I travelled east to Africa, across the Atlantic Ocean;
>And in the jungle I did see — a long-nosed, fat anteater,
>With a flp, flp, Yum! and a flp, flp, Yum!
>Here a flp, there a flp, everywhere a Yum! Yum!
>*Refrain* (Repeat first line of song)
>And in the jungle I did see — crocodiles in the river,
>With a (yawn) here, and a (yawn) there,
>Here a (yawn), there a (yawn), everywhere a (YAWN),
>A flp, flp, Yum! and a flp, flp, Yum!
>Here a flp, there a flp, everywhere a Yum! Yum!
>*Refrain* (Repeat first line of song)
>And in the jungle I did see — monkeys in the treetops,
>With a scratch, scratch here, and a scratch, scratch there
>Here a scratch, there a scratch, everywhere a scratch, scratch,
>A (yawn) here, and a (yawn) there,
>Here a (yawn), there a (yawn), everywhere a (YAWN),
>A flp, flp, Yum! and a flp, flp, Yum!
>Here a flp, there a flp, everywhere a Yum! Yum!
>*Refrain* (Repeat first line of song)

Expand and Create

List other animals of the African jungle.

Have students create verses as a class, then on their own.
>(What did you see? What did it do?)

Write them on the board and sing them.

Rewrite the song for Asia and South America.
>(Find Asia on the map. How could we get there?)
>(What other animals might you see?)

Compose a new refrain and verses.

"*I flew my plane around the world
To see the Asian jungle.*"

"*I sailed to South America
To see its big rain forest.*"

Products of the Tropical Forests

Many people ask, "Since I don't live in the tropics, what does the rain forest have to do with me?" That's a good question. If you live in a house or apartment, wash your hair, eat fruits and vegetables, need medicines, chew gum or wear sneakers, chances are you may be using products that originated in the tropical forests.

Tropical plants have been used to treat many illnesses of the world's population. Quinine treats malaria. A West African vine is medication for leukemia and Hodgkin's disease. In fact, of the 3,000 plant species in the world that are known to contain anti-cancer properties, 2,100 are from the tropical rain forests. These plants can save lives! Scientists have been able to look at less than one percent of the tropical plants for medical purposes. So, many more medical uses may be discovered.

Remember those Tarzan films, in which the tribes used blow darts to defeat their enemies? The poison on the darts, curare, is an important anesthetic used to relax muscles during surgery.

Natural rubber comes from rain forest areas. For many uses, only natural rubber from trees will do. Rubber gives us surgical gloves, balloons, bandaids, sporting goods, sneakers, and chewing gum. Imagine a world without sneakers and bubble gum!

From tropical plants we get fibers for things like furniture, soundproofing, and insulation. From palm oil we get ingredients for margarine, cooking oil, bakery goods, soap, candles, and mayonnaise.

Foods that we now take for granted originated in the jungle. Today these are grown as crops and include bananas, rice, avocados, eggplant, lemons, limes, oranges, cucumbers, tea, cashews, pineapples, and papayas. Spices like black pepper, chili, cinnamon, cloves, vanilla, paprika, ginger, and nutmeg originated in the rain forest. Our tropical rain forests have given us an abundance of foods and spices.

Activities

1. Make a rain forest products collage.

2. Research to find other products that originated in the jungle.

3. Make a product map to show which rain forests the products come from.

54

Products Related to the Rain Forest

fruits
vegetables
chewing gum
rubber
furniture
insulation
soundproofing
margarine
cooking oil
soap
candles
mayonnaise
bandaids
sneakers
medicines

bananas
rice
avocados
eggplant
lemons
limes
chili
cinnamon
cloves
vanilla
quinine
pineapples
balloons
curare

```
C M A V A C A D O S A S D K T A S
X C S R E K A E N S D I A D N A B N J
Q H J L S D F N Q W E R T Y A S D F O G H
U C J F O G H D H R W W E L I M E S O H O
D I O K R L V I L J U E F P I O J O M L N I
F N O U U T R E E G B R G S D G H I N L K U
G I K Q I W E R S F B G H J K L V U B A A Y
H N I W T T F Y U I E Q W E R U E Y V B S T
C E N E S O U N D P R O O F I N G T C C D R
H S G R D F R S E S I K T A N G E R X I F E
E I O T Z F N N F G C S Y E S D T E Z N G W
W A I A X S I H D H E C U R U S A N A N A B
I N L Y P R T V A N I L L A L M B W Z A C A
N N N U A E U G S J E I I E A I L Q A M H S
G O H G C E R A R U C O M Y T U E A S O I D
G Y R I V U E F S K D O O U I Y S S D N L
U A U O B I E D A L N T K I O T R D F K I
M M E D I C I N E S Q W E R N E T F G L S
S D P F S E L P P A E N I P R E G H O
```

The Panama Canal

Planning a cruise from New York to California? Trying to ship goods from Europe to San Francisco? You will probably want to use the Panama Canal, the shortcut between the Atlantic Ocean and the Pacific Ocean.

Tropical deforestation, the destruction of the rain forests, threatens the Panama Canal. Scientists predict that 40% of the Canal's reservoir will be filled with silt by the year 2000. As Panama's forests are cut down to make room for more people and farming, the trees no longer prevent the loss of top soil during the rainy season. Therefore, the soil is washed away, much of it finally ending up in the Canal.

Use a blue crayon to mark the route from New York to San Francisco by way of the Panama Canal. Use a red crayon to mark the New York – San Francisco route around the tip of South America. Why is the Panama Canal important? Write your answer on the back of this paper.

Extension: Research alternate routes from New York City to San Francisco and compare the distances and the costs.

Vanishing Songbirds

As the South and Central American rain forests are cut down, some species of North American songbirds that fly south to winter in the rain forests also decline.

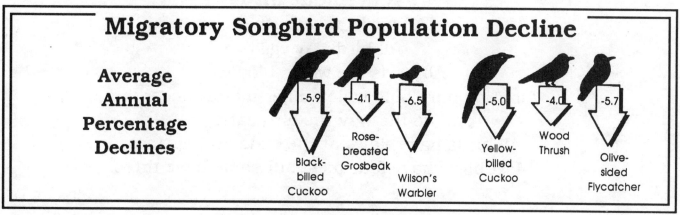

Multiply the above percentages by 10 to complete the graph below.

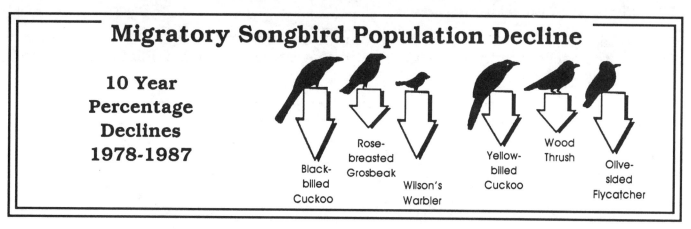

Complete the following chart by doubling the 1978-1987 percentages to project what will happen by the year 2000. Over 100% means the species will become extinct! Color blue the arrows of those that may be extinct.

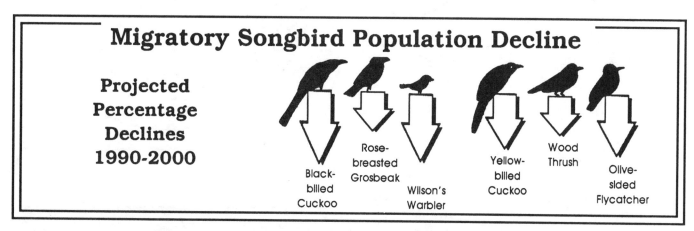

Extension: Write a newspaper editorial citing facts and pleading the songbirds' case. Put it in *The Jungle Journal* (page 46).

Create a Bird

Birds of the jungle are often very colorful and beautiful. A peacock and a parrot are jungle birds.

Facts About Birds
All birds have feathers.
All birds lay eggs.
All birds are warm-blooded.
All birds have bills which differ mainly according
to the way the bird eats.
All birds have claws at the ends of their toes.
Most birds have four toes, but some have three.

Use these facts, the shapes below, feathers, paper scraps, and your imagination to create an undiscovered jungle bird.

On a separate sheet of paper, assemble your bird. Add lots of detail. Make it colorful. Draw in the background. Give your newly discovered bird a name. Fill in a Specimen Report (page 12).

Extension: Use this same method to create your own jungle mammals and fish. Add these new species of animals to the collection of insects you created when you read *Why Mosquitoes Buzz in People's Ears.*

58

The Greenhouse Effect

Box 1

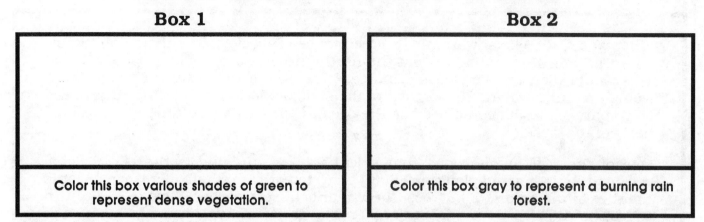

Color this box various shades of green to represent dense vegetation.

Box 2

Color this box gray to represent a burning rain forest.

Box 1 represents a photo taken of the Amazon Basin from *Skylab 2* in 1973. Box 2 represents the same area 15 years later in a photo taken from the *Space Shuttle*. Dense smoke from the burning of the rain forests completely covered the ground. The cloud of smoke was large enough to cover the entire state of Texas three times!

The burning of the rain forests to make room for agriculture, cattle, and population growth adds extra carbon dioxide to our atmosphere. (So do the traffic jams on our highways!) Scientists believe that more carbon dioxide in our atmosphere will make the earth warmer. Trees and other green plants absorb carbon dioxide (CO_2) and give off oxygen. So, burning the earth's forests is double trouble. Not only does the burning itself add CO_2 to the atmosphere, but when the trees are gone, they can no longer absorb the excess CO_2 or make the oxygen animals need to breathe.

The more CO_2 in the atmosphere, the more heat is trapped in our atmosphere and the warmer the earth becomes. This is called the **Greenhouse Effect**. NASA's Goddard Institute for Space Studies predicts that by the year 2050 most of the world will experience warmer weather. Here is how the **Greenhouse Effect** works. The sun's light passes through the Earth's atmosphere. The energy of the sunlight is radiated back out into space in the form of heat. Not all the heat escapes. Some of it is trapped by the atmosphere which works like a blanket. As more CO_2 is added to the atmosphere, the blanket becomes thicker. Less heat goes into space.

Color the sun and its rays yellow.

Color the atmosphere blue.

Color the earth brown.

Color the escaping heat red.

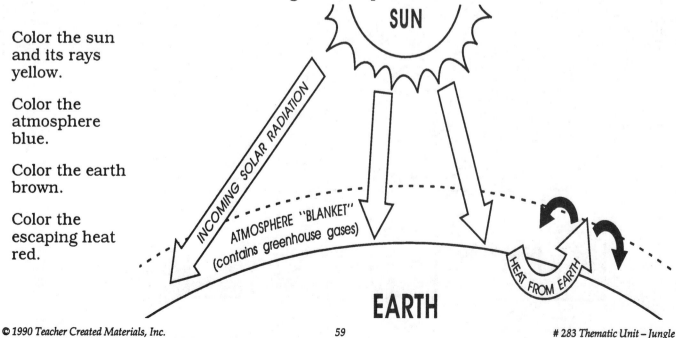

The Greenhouse Effect *(cont.)*

What would the global warming or greenhouse effect do? Scientists don't know for sure. Scientists do agree that the northern polar areas will warm the most. This would melt the ice cap and increase the size of the ocean. Coastal areas would be under water. Since much of the state of Florida is near the current sea level, part of Florida could become the ocean floor. This would be true in many parts of the world.

One of the biggest questions that scientists are studying is the effect global warming could have on plankton. Plant plankton are the small microscopic plants that live in the ocean. Like trees, these plants absorb carbon dioxide and return oxygen to the air. Giant masses of plankton thrive in our oceans. A change in the amount of plankton caused by global warming could significantly affect the amounts of carbon dioxide and oxygen in our atmosphere.

Below is a map of the world's plankton. Color the continents brown. Color the plankton areas green. Color the remainder of the ocean blue. Remember to color your key as well. This should give you a good idea of the tremendous importance of plankton to the carbon dioxide/oxygen cycle.

The World's Plankton

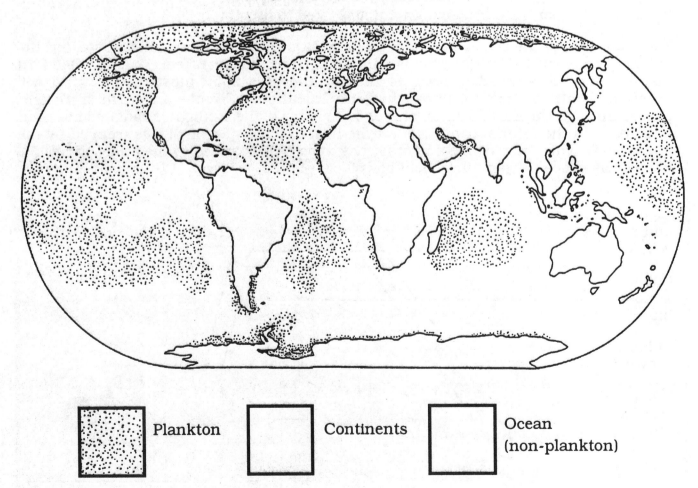

Plankton   Continents   Ocean (non-plankton)

The Vanishing Rain Forest

Each minute of each day, an area of rain forest the size of 10 city blocks vanishes from the Earth.* Use a calculator to complete the following tables to find out how much rain forest disappears each year. (**Note:** Measurements are approximate and rounded. Do not write in gray areas.)

Table 1

1 minute	10 blocks
2 minutes	20 blocks
3 minutes	
4 minutes	
5 minutes	
6 minutes	
7 minutes	
8 minutes	
9 minutes	
10 minutes	
60 minutes	

Table 3

1 day	192 sq. miles (312 sq. km)
2 days	
3 days	
4 days	
5 days	
6 days	
7 days	

Table 2

1 hour	600 blocks	8 sq. miles (13 sq. km)
2 hours		
3 hours		
4 hours		
5 hours		
6 hours		
12 hours		
24 hours		

Table 4

1 week	1,344 sq. miles (2,184 sq. km)
2 weeks	
3 weeks	
4 weeks	
5 weeks	
10 weeks	
50 weeks	
52 weeks	

About how much rain forest vanishes each year? _____

rounded to nearest 10,000

***American Forests**, Nov. - Dec., 1988*

The Vanishing Rain Forest *(cont.)*

The latest estimate is that the world is losing approximately 60,000 to 70,000 square miles (114,000 sq. km) of rain forest per year. This is equal to **an area about the size of the state of Washington!**

Use a calculator and fill in the chart below:

YEARS	SQUARE MILES LOST	APPROXIMATE AREA COMPARED TO THE U.S.A.
1	70,000 (114,000 sq. km)	STATE OF WASHINGTON
5		
10		ALL STATES WEST OF THE ROCKIES
15		
20		
25		
30		ALL STATES WEST OF THE MISSISSIPPI RIVER
35		
40		
45		ALL STATES WEST OF THE APPALACHIAN MOUNTAINS
50		ALL STATES IN THE CONTINENTAL U.S.A.

Imagine that the U.S.A. is a rain forest. On a map, shade the areas that **disappear** at 1, 10, 30, 45, and 50 years in different colors. Make a key at the bottom to explain.

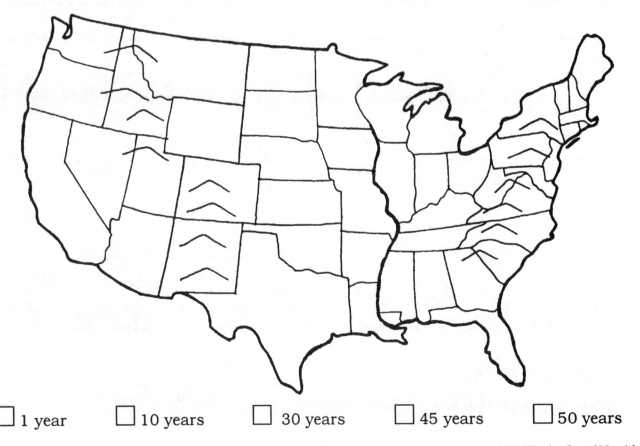

☐ 1 year   ☐ 10 years   ☐ 30 years   ☐ 45 years   ☐ 50 years

The Hamburger Connection

The reasons for destruction of the world's rain forests are varied. There are a combination of logging, cattle ranching, and other economic factors.

In Central America, cattle ranching is the major factor. What do you get when you clear a rain forest? HAMBURGERS! Two-thirds of Central American agricultural land is used to grow beef. Most of the beef goes to the U.S.A. to make fast-food hamburgers.

It takes about 50 square feet (4.5 sq. m) of converted rain forest land over a period of eight years to produce one hamburger!

Activity:

On your school playground, measure and mark off (use string or playing field chalk) a 50 square foot (4.5 sq. m) area for each person in your class.

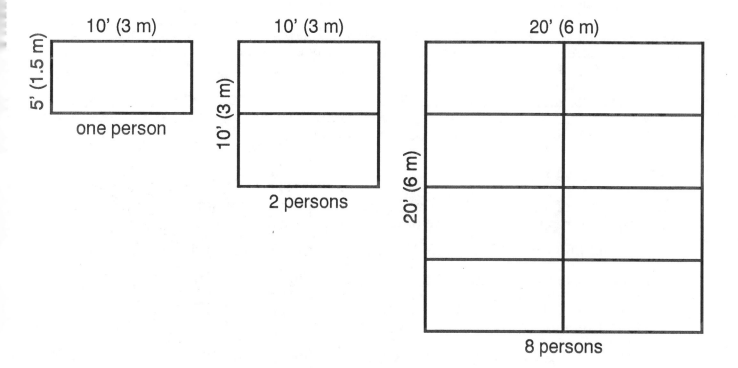

Now, imagine that all this land will be used for nothing but grazing cows for eight years. At the end of that time it will produce one hamburger for each class member — only one lunch! Is this a wise use of land? Write a thoughtful answer to this question, remembering that the land would be rain forest if it had not been cleared for raising cattle.

The Carnival of the Animals

Camille Saint-Saens (San Sawns) was a French composer. He was born in Paris in 1835. Camille reacted to musical sounds in his infancy. As a child, he was recognized as a prodigy.

A beautiful tone made his face shine.

A discord made him cry.

He began piano lessons when he was two and a half. He completed his first piano book in only one month! When he was four and a half he had his first performance. He played music written by Beethoven. At age five he was already composing songs and piano pieces.

Even though he was very famous, he had a lot of sadness in his lifetime. In one year, his two-year-old child fell out of a window and was killed. His second child died suddenly a few weeks later.

Saint-Saens loved to travel. He visited Russia, Egypt, South America, and the United States. He composed and performed until he was eighty-six. When he died, there was a national day of mourning in France.

He wrote many, many compositions. The most famous are "Danse Macabre" (The Dance of Death) and "The Carnival of the Animals." Camille wrote the second piece just for his own fun. He would never let it be performed in his lifetime, but you will get to hear it!

Responding to the music:

"The Carnival of the Animals" is a stimulating piece of music. Children should be encouraged to respond to it in one of the following ways:

1. List and illustrate the animals that the music brings to mind.

2. Make an abstract painting that recreates the mood called forth by the music.

3. Create movements or a dance for all or part of the music. This dance may include animal-like movements.

4. Write a mood poem from a list of describing words made while listening to "The Carnival of the Animals."

For example: Galloping, frolicking, playful — light.

Slowing, walking, resting — night.

Yummy Yams

Ingredients	Equipment

Ingredients

1 large can yams
1 small can crushed pineapple
1 cup (250 mL) miniature marshmallows
2 tbsp. (30 mL) butter or margarine, melted

Equipment

can opener
potato masher
2 qt. (2 L) casserole dish
oven
large spoon

❶ Preheat the oven to 350°F (190°C).

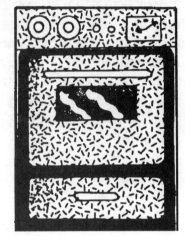

❷ Open the cans and drain off the liquid.

❸ Mash the yams and pineapple together with a potato masher.

❹ Add butter or margarine and stir.

❺ Sprinkle marshmallows on top of yam mix.

❻ Bake for 20-25 minutes.

Serves eight.

Eat and enjoy!

A Taste of the Tropics

Tropical Tasting Party

Many students will not have tasted the tropical fruits, nuts, and juices that are now fairly common in supermarkets. Arrange to have a tasting party. Have students bring in fresh papayas, mangoes, passion fruits, kiwis, pineapples, bananas, coconuts, cashews, etc. Juices of these fruits alone or in combinations may also be added. Have students help clean, peel, and cut the fruits into bite-size portions. Arrange them attractively and then taste and enjoy. Students may find new flavors to appreciate!

The monkey shake and frozen bananas below may also be served at the party.

Monkey Shake (for 2 people)*

INGREDIENTS: Vanilla ice cream; milk; banana; 1/2 cup (125 mL) chopped dates (optional)

EQUIPMENT: Blender; ice cream scoop; cups

DIRECTIONS: Put two scoops of vanilla ice cream in blender. Add enough milk to cover the ice cream. Peel the banana and place it in the blender. Add chopped dates, if desired. Blend on HIGH until ingredients are mixed. (If you have added dates, mixture will be chunky.)

*   *For each additional person, add one more scoop of vanilla ice cream and 1/2 banana to ingredients in the blender.*

Frozen Chocolate Nut Bananas (for 2 people)

INGREDIENTS: 1/4 cup (65 mL) chopped nuts; 1/2 cup (125 mL) chocolate pieces; 1 banana, cut in half

EQUIPMENT: Measuring cups; wax paper; plates; small pan; wooden spoon; knife; two wooden skewers

DIRECTIONS: Spread the nuts on a plate. Melt the chocolate pieces over low heat, stirring constantly with wooden spoon. Push a skewer into the cut end of each banana half. With the knife, spread chocolate on all sides of the banana. Roll the bananas in the nuts. Place the bananas on a wax paper-lined plate; freeze just until they're hard. For variety, roll the bananas in coconut instead of nuts.

Animals Talk Back

A RESEARCH CENTER ON ENDANGERED SPECIES

Objective

The purpose of this center is to build awareness of global environmental issues. The destruction of our environment is not just a problem confined to the jungle. In the United States the national symbol, the bald eagle, is on the verge of extinction.

At this center students can work individually or in pairs to read, write, and talk about endangered animals. It provides a simple method of note taking, a way to write a report without copying from the book, and a fun and non-threatening method for doing an oral presentation.

Preparation

Make the center. (See page 68.) Once it is assembled, save it and you are all set for the next class.

Collect reading material on endangered animals. *Ranger Rick Magazine* is an excellent source. See the bibliography (page 79) for additional suggestions.

Allow six to ten working periods of 30-45 minutes for completion of all the activities. Some of these can be designated for homework.

Procedure

1. Introduce the center to the class. Have students select the animal that they wish to study. Distribute and explain "Writing Note Cards" (page 71).

2. Distribute and model "Writing a Bibliography" (page 72). Allow time for students to read and record data. This can be done during reading time, assigned as homework, or a combination.

3. Distribute "Animals Talk Back" (pages 73-74). Again, model this activity for the best results. Allow time for students to complete this activity in class or at home.

4. Distribute "Putting It All Together" (page 75). Read it over with all the students. Allow time for students to make folders, do map, illustrate, proofread, and assemble their reports.

5. Distribute "Table of Contents" (page 76). Have students fill out and add to their folders.

6. Distribute "Making An Oral Presentation: An Animal Interview" (page 78). Allow time for students to make the animal mask and practice their oral presentation. (The mask could be done as homework to build parent awareness and save class time.)

Students give oral presentations to the class. These can be video-taped or photographed to make a great display for Parent Night!

Endangered Species
Research Center

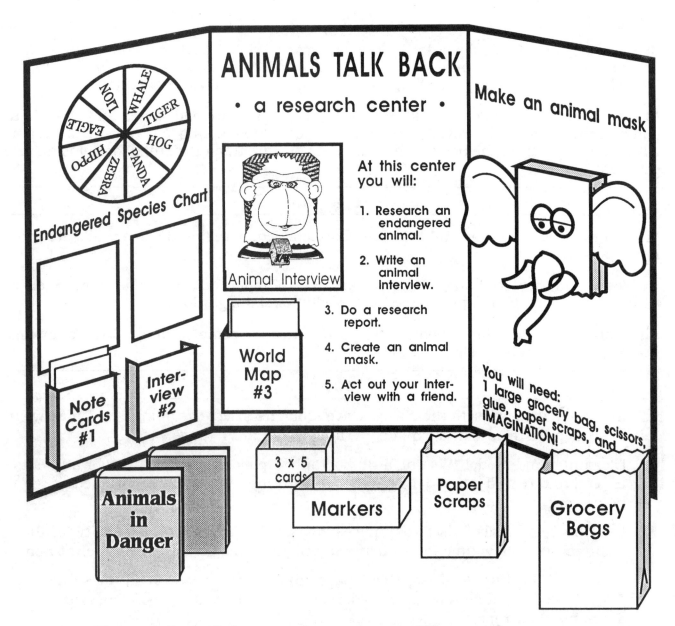

To make this center you will need:

- 3 sheets poster board
- 3 9" X 12" mailing envelopes
- 1 large grocery bag per student
- 8 3" X 5" lined index cards per student
- lots of paper scraps
- markers
- books and magazines on endangered animals (see Bibliography for partial list)

- 1 Endangered Species Chart
- 1 Animal Interview Picture (page 70)
- Writing Note Cards (page 71), 1 per student.
- Animal Interview (page 73 and 74), 1 set per student
- World Map (page 77), 1 per student

68

Endangered Species Chart

1. Cut out.

2. Mount on heavy paper.

3. Use brad to attach to left side of Learning Center.

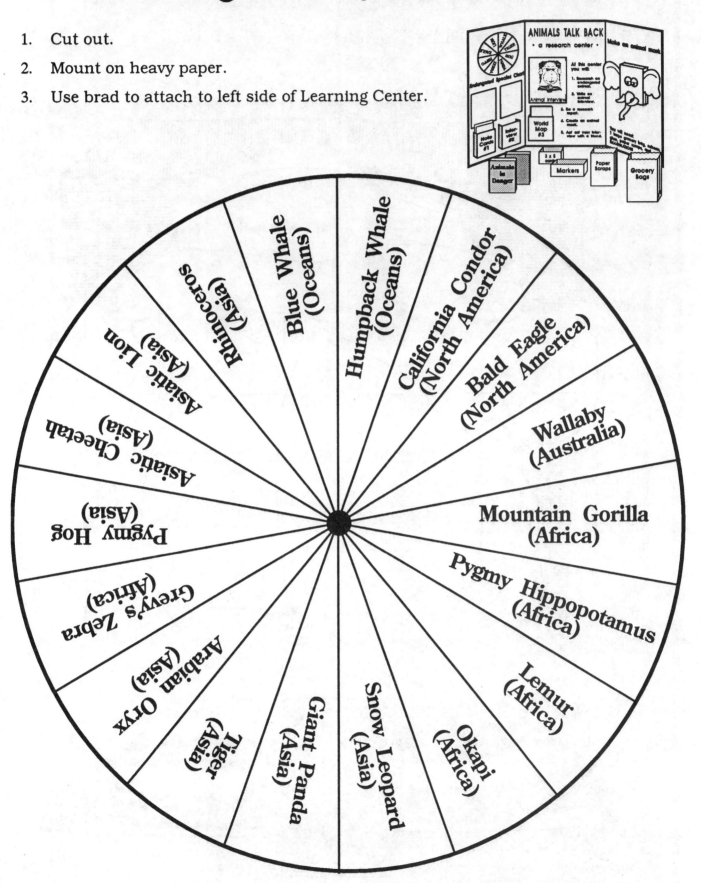

The wheel contains the following sections:

- Blue Whale (Oceans)
- Humpback Whale (Oceans)
- California Condor (North America)
- Bald Eagle (North America)
- Wallaby (Australia)
- Mountain Gorilla (Africa)
- Pygmy Hippopotamus (Africa)
- Lemur (Africa)
- Okapi (Africa)
- Snow Leopard (Asia)
- Giant Panda (Asia)
- Tiger (Asia)
- Arabian Oryx (Asia)
- Grevy's Zebra (Africa)
- Pygmy Hog (Asia)
- Asiatic Cheetah (Asia)
- Asiatic Lion (Asia)
- Rhinoceros (Asia)

Animal Interview Picture

1. Reproduce on heavy paper.

2. Color and cut out.

3. Attach to middle section of center.

70

Name _____

Writing a Research Report: Note Cards

First: The first step in a research report is deciding what you want to learn about. Select one of the endangered animals from the wheel.

I have decided to learn about _____.

Second: The next step is to read about your animal and take notes. You do not want to copy word for word from the book. This is like stealing someone else's words. It is called plagiarism.

Make for your notes.

* Cut out the topics listed below.

* Glue each on a 3" X 5" (7 X 12 cm) note card.

* When you read a fact on that topic, write it on the card.

* Keep all the cards in an envelope so you don't lose them.

What it eats (Food)

Name and description	**Where it lives (Habitat)**
What it eats (Food)	**How it reproduces**
How it raises its young	**How it protects itself**
What are its enemies	**Why it is endangered**
Other interesting facts	**Other interesting facts**

Name _____

Writing a Research Report: Bibliography

You need to keep track of the books and magazines you read. When you write something on your note cards, write down the information about the book or magazine it came from. Be sure to record this information before you take the book back to the library! This is called a **Bibliography**.

Use the format below for your **Bibliography**.

Remember: A good research paper uses more than just one source!

Book

_____ , _____
author's last name   author's first name

_____
name of the book

_____
publisher

_____ , _____
pages you read   date book was copyrighted ©

Magazine

_____ , _____
author's last name   author's first name

" _____ "
name of the article

_____
name of the magazine

_____ , _____
pages   month and year

---

* **Teacher Note:** *These may be reproduced on heavy paper so students may cut apart and store with note cards.*

Writing a Research Report:
Animal Interview

Now your notes are finished. You have learned a lot about your animal. Pretend you are a reporter. Pretend your animal can talk! You are going to interview your animal for "Animals Talk Back" — a TV show about animal rights.

Complete pages 73 and 74 for your report (page 75) and oral presentation (page 78).

Animals Talk Back

An Interview with a (an) _____
(your animal)

     by reporter _____ .
(your name)

I'm here in _____ with an endangered species. Could you please
(continent)

describe yourself for our readers? _____

_____

_____

Tell us about your habitat. _____

_____

_____

_____

What are your favorite foods? _____

_____

_____

How are your young born? _____

_____

_____

Animal Interview (cont.)

How do you take care of your young? _____

_____

_____

_____

Who are your natural enemies? _____

_____

_____

_____

How can you protect yourself? _____

_____

_____

_____

I know you are an endangered species. What are the main reasons for that? _____

_____

_____

_____

We have a nationwide audience in the millions. What else would you like to tell us about yourself?

_____

_____

_____

_____

_____

_____

_____

Writing a Research Report: Putting It All Together

Most of your work is done, but putting it together neatly is also important!

1. Get or make a folder for your report. On the front put the title, your name, and the date.

2. Make a title page. This is the same as the folder cover but it's on the first page.

3. Put the Table of Contents (page 76) next. Fill in the page numbers when your report is completely assembled.

4. Next put in your Animal Interview. Be sure someone has checked it for neatness and spelling. Recopy it if necessary. A messy paper looks like you don't really care about your animal.

5. Add a map to show where your animal lives. Get a world map (page 77) from the Research Center. Label the continent(s) and color the part where your animal lives.

6. Add illustrations. Draw several pictures of your animal and label them. Put them after the map.

7. The last page is the Bibliography. This is a list of the books you used. Use page 72 to help with the form.

Endangered Species

Table of Contents

(and check off sheet)

Title page .... page ___ ☐

Table of Contents .... page ___ ☐

Interview with Endangered Animal ..... page ___ ☐

Map .... page ___ ☐

Illustrations .... page ___ ☐

Bibliography..................................... page ___ ☐

(student checks if complete)

Grade expected: _____

(student fills out)

Grade received: _____

(teacher fills out)

Comments: _____

(teacher fills out)

_____

_____

Writing A Research Report: World Map

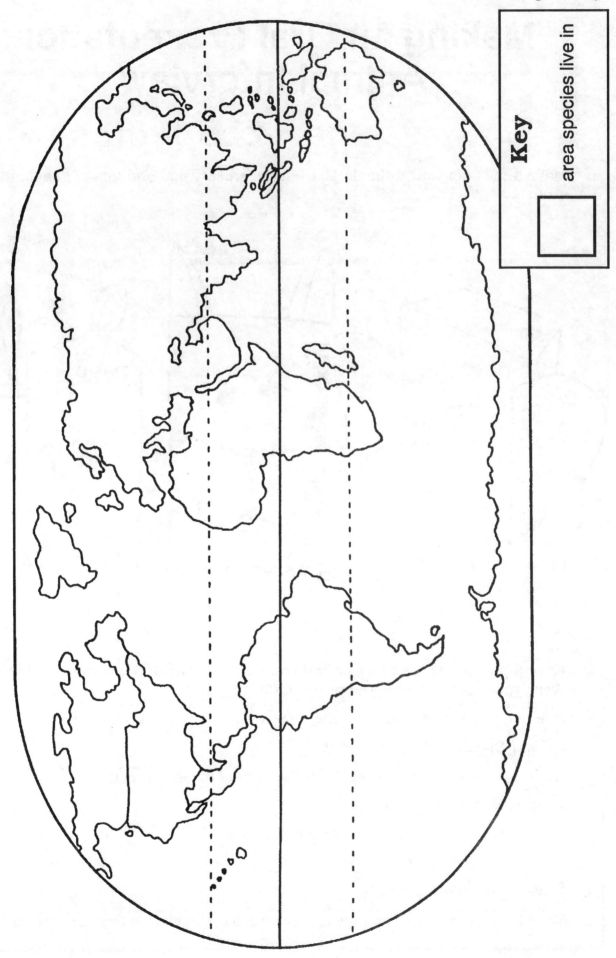

Key

area species live in

Making an Oral Presentation:
Animal Interview

1. Make a mask of your animal. Use a large grocery bag and lots of imagination.

2. Have a partner be the reporter and you play the part of the endangered animal. Wear your mask for the final presentation.

3. Practice reading your animal interview from your report. Be sure you:

    a. Speak slowly and clearly.

    b. Speak loudly (especially in the animal mask).

    c. Memorize your part.

    d. Say something interesting in a powerful manner for the final question.

    e. Practice a lot.

4. Have a good time!

5. Your teacher may wish to tape (audio or video) your interview to share with others.

Bibliography

Children's Books on Jungles and Rain Forests

Baker, Jeannie. *Where the Forest Meets the Sea.* Greenwillow, 1987

Cowcher, Helen. *Rain Forests.* Farrar, 1988

Forsyth, Adrian. *Journey Through a Tropical Jungle.* Simon and Schuster, 1989

George, Jean Craighead. *One Day in the Tropical Rain Forest.* Crowell, 1990

Moore, Chris. *The Jungles: A Science Activity Book.* Puffin, 1988

National Wildlife Staff (ed. Victor Waldrop). *Wonders of the Jungle.* National Wildlife, 1986

Rowland-Entwhistle. *Jungles and Rainforests.* Silver, Burdett, and Ginn, 1987

Books on Endangered Species

Burgess, Jeremy. *Just Look At. . .Endangered Earth.* Rourke Enterprises, 1988

Burton, John. *Close to Extinction.* Gloucester Press, 1988

Gould, Gill. *Animals in Danger: Asia* (and others in the series). The Rourke Corporation, Windermere, 1982

Stone, Lynn M. *A New True Book: Endangered Animals.* Children's Press, 1984

Stuart, Gene S. *Wildlife Alert! The Struggle to Survive.* National Geographic Society, 1980

Whitcombe, Bobbie. *Animals in Danger.* Brimax Books, 1988

Related Fiction Books for Children

Aardema, Verna. *Bimiwili and the Zimwi.* Dial, 1985

Aardema, Verna. *Oh, Kojo! How Could You!* Dial, 1988

Aardema, Verna. *Why Mosquitoes Buzz in People's Ears.* Dial, 1975

DeBrunhoff, Jean. *The Story of Babar* (and others in the series). Random, 1984

Haley, Gail E. *A Story, A Story.* Macmillan, 1970

Harris, Joel C. (Adapted by Van D. Parks and Malcolm Jones). *Jump: The Adventures of Brer Rabbit.* HBJ, 1986

Harris, Joel C. (Adapted by Barry Moser). *Jump Again! More Adventures of Brer Rabbit.* HBJ, 1987

Kimmel, Eric A. (retold by). *Anansi and the Moss-Covered Rock.* Holiday, 1988

McDermott, Gerald (retold by). *Anansi the Spider: A Tale from the Ashanti.* Holt, 1972

Rey, H.A. *Curious George* (and others in the series). Houghton Mifflin, 1973

Sherlock, Phillip K. *Anansi, the Spider Man.* Harper, 1954

Poetry Books

Prelutsky, Jack (selected by). *The Random House Book of Poetry for Children.* Random House, 1983

Silverstein, Shel. *Where the Sidewalk Ends.* Harper, 1974

Teacher References

American Forests Magazine. November/December, 1988

Los Angeles Times. "Rain Forest Going Faster Than Feared" June 8, 1990, pages A1 and A42

Los Angeles Times. "Pennies for the Planet" April 25, 1990, pages B1 and B3

Monasstersky, R. "Carbon Dioxide: Where Does It All Go?" *Science News: The Weekly Magazine of Science.* Volume 1136, no. 9, August 26, 1989, page 132

Answer Key

Page 8 and 9

Animal	Picture	Action	Sound
Iguana		went off through the reeds	mek, mek, mok
Iguana		bobbing its head	badamin, badamin
Python		slithering	wasawusu
Rabbit		bounded	krik, krik, krik
Crow		crying	kaa, kaa, kaa
Monkey		screeching and leaping	kili wili
All animals		came and sat down	pem, pem, pem
Monkey		glancing from side to side	rim, rim, rim, rim
Mother Owl		hooted	Hool Hooooo!
Lion		laughed	nge, nge, nge

Page 27

H, B, G, C, K, E, J, I, F, A, D

Page 47

1. equator
2. South America
3. Asian
4. too cool, not enough rain

Page 55

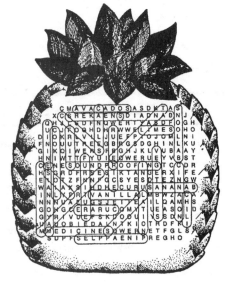

Page 56

The canal provides a shorter, less costly route.

Page 57

1978-1987   59 41 65 50 40 57

1990-2000   118 82 130 100 80 114

Page 61

1. 20 blocks
    30 blocks
    40 blocks
    50 blocks
    60 blocks
    70 blocks
    80 blocks
    90 blocks
    100 blocks
    600 blocks

2. 1200 blocks/16 sq.mi./26 sq.km
    1800 blocks/24 sq.mi./39 sq.km
    2400 blocks/32 sq.mi./52 sq.km
    3000 blocks/40 sq.mi./65 sq.km
    3600 blocks/48 sq.mi./78 sq.km
    6000 blocks/96 sq.mi./156 sq.km
    12,000 blocks/192 sq.mi./312 sq.km

3. 384 sq.mi/624 sq.km
    576 sq.mi/936 sq.km
    768 sq.mi/1248 sq.km
    960 sq.mi/1560 sq.km
    1152 sq.mi/1872 sq.km
    1344 sq.mi/2184 sq.km

4. 2688 sq.mi./4368 sq.km
    4032 sq.mi./6552 sq.km
    5376 sq.mi./8736 sq.km
    6720 sq.mi./10,920 sq.km
    13,440 sq.mi./21,840 sq.km
    67,200 sq.mi./109,200 sq.km
    69,888 sq.mi./113,568 sq.km
    each year = 70,000 sq.mi. rounded to nearest 10,000 (114,000 sq.km)

Page 62

5 yrs = 350,000 sq.mi./570,000 sq.km

10 yrs = 700,000 sq.mi./1,140,000 sq.km

15 yrs = 1,050,000 sq.mi./1,710,000 sq.km

20 yrs = 1,400,000 sq.mi./2,280,000 sq.km

25 yrs = 1,750,000 sq.mi./2,850,000 sq.km

30 yrs = 2,100,000 sq.mi./3,420,000 sq.km

35 yrs = 2,450,000 sq.mi./3,990,000 sq.km

40 yrs = 2,800,000 sq.mi./4,560,000 sq.km

45 yrs = 3,150,000 sq.mi./5,130,000 sq.km

50 yrs = 3,500,000 sq.mi./5,700,000 sq.km